AF251281

TOWARDS HUMAN UNITY

Towards Human UNITY

by Anthony Brooke

The Mitre Press
52 Lincoln's Inn Fields · London
in collaboration with
Foundation for Peace through Unity
Gövik · Särö · Sweden

© ANTHONY BROOKE, 1976
ISBN 0 7051 0234 3
Printed in Gt. Britain for The Mitre Press
(Fudge & Co. Ltd.), London.

CONTENTS

Introduction

Mighty changes are taking place in the consciousness of man and in the world which he is creating in his likeness around him. It is only when viewed within the context of the wider pattern of an epochal transition affecting not only our planet and solar system but the entire universal scheme of things, that the chaos and confusion which so many are experiencing begin to be seen in a meaningful perspective which gives them a creative significance. They are in fact inevitable ingredients of the overall process as the pent-up energy within old forms, whether they be thought forms or their counterpart in the world of manifestation, achieves release to make way for the new. A dynamic universe, in which all is constant motion, cannot long tolerate unchanging states; and the cessation of our suffering depends upon our willingness consciously to de-identify from attachment to the many forms—credal, social, cultural, racial, political, ideological and economic—to *re-identify with our inner divinity,* and then consciously and creatively to flow with the constructive universal energies of dynamic change which are making all things new.

The contents of this book centre around the *fact* of ever accelerating change in the universe with which life on earth in its many forms, human and otherwise, is confronted and invites attention to the many different ways open to man to become informed about and to respond to the to the necessity for inner transformation so that he may move with the changes and participate effectively in the new world that is coming to birth: what is even more important, that he may himself become a conscious creator of this new world.

The pages which follow attempt to throw light on what is happening and what is being offered to man at this time. Although from his contacts, experiences and understanding the writer no more than touches the bare fringe of these universal developments, some names and addresses are to be found within these pages and in the appendix which it is hoped may assist the reader to follow up any particular lines of approach and understanding to which he may feel drawn.

Most of what is here written was initially given in the form of a series of talks to groups of different kinds, the first six chapters having appeared in *Revelation for the New Age,* now out of print.

It is to be hoped that publication in the present form may serve as useful study material for individuals and groups and as an elementary introduction to aspects of our changing times regarding which the attitude of our governments and educational institutions remains somewhat reserved. It should perhaps be added that, by the very nature of the theme which has preoccupied the writer, this compilation inevitably throws light on his own spiritual pilgrimage over the period of ten years during which these selected talks were given, and the discerning reader will observe a movement in consciousness which there has been no attempt to disguise.

Two chapters of this book are devoted to the Universal Link Revelation. Readers will interpret what this signifies according to their own insight and understanding. *Revelation—the Birth of a New Age,* by David Spangler, was written when the author was living in the Findhorn Community (now the Findhorn University of Light) and was the first book to be published there. This writer recommends it as providing both an elucidation and a clarification of the Universal Link Revelation. It also contains some notable insights into our changing times and what is signified by the term *the New Age.* The following example of a revealed insight from this book challenges many outworn concepts regarding ways to achieve peace:

> "Man will not find peace on human level explorations, for he has no conception of what peace requires nor of what it demands of him. Peace is deeper than a simple cessation of conflict; peace is not the opposite of war. Peace is life and life abundantly overflowing its limitations. Peace is vital. Peace is growth. Peace is what I am. Seek Me and you have found peace."

More insights into the ramifications of this global operation are to be found in the publications of Merta Mary Parkinson of the Dena Foundation and in *Exploring the Mysteries of Life,* the outcome of thirty years of spiritual and psychical research, by Nellie B. Cain.

Mention must also be made of the movement Universal World Harmony, a direct offspring and expression of the Universal Link operation. This movement is becoming an increasingly unifying influence through its outreach into many countries and all continents by reason of its approach to unity and peace through a simple formula of conscious attunement in which all may readily participate.

Prominent among other world wide peace movements are World Union, with its global outreach based upon the work and programme of the Sri Aurobindo Ashram, Pondicherry, India; also World Goodwill, which for many years has published excellent and highly informative material relating to world service in this time of transition into a new age. The Movement of Unity, with its international headquarters in Missouri, U.S.A., is an equally notable unifying spiritual force with growing influence throughout many countries.

The writer has alluded to his own spiritual pilgrimage and wishes here to express his deep thankfulness to countless individuals and groups of individuals whom he has met along the way and who, together with life in its many other forms, have been his teachers. Among these have been gurus of India and those in many lands who make no such claim, yet who consciously and often unconsciously have taught him valuable lessons. Above and beyond all, the teaching of the inner light claims preeminence and it is this which has now led him to work for unity and peace from this focal point in Scandinavia.

The challenging contact with the Holy Spirit Association for the Unification of World Christianity, especially in the course of two visits to Korea, helped greatly to stimulate and strengthen his sense of personal spiritual responsibility.

An experience of spiritual intimacy with that exemplary community, the Emissaries of Divine Light, especially throughout a month-long study course taken at their international headquarters in the spring of 1970, left a lasting impact in the deepening of the writer's commitment and sense of true identity.

As the result of some memorable visits at crucial moments in his life, he feels a special affinity with the Institute of Crystal Truths (the Mu-Ne-Dowk Foundation), with its wide open universal vision and for all that is unfolding there.

And throughout all this time the Findhorn Community—that spiritual cauldron of dynamic transformation with its ever spreading influence and light—provided a base from which the writer moved out on missions of linking and sharing, returning there from time to time to renew his energies. How the heart overflows with joy and thankfulness for so many wondrous experiences and for the awareness that mankind is everywhere being awakened and offered so many possibilities of transformation and of rebuilding the world!

An eminent astronomer once exclaimed, "something unknown is doing we don't know what"! Others boldly acknowledge the reality of a supreme and loving power and intelligence permeating all life. It is hoped that what is revealed within these pages may serve to bear witness to the truth of a loving creator whose Presence infuses and supports all life; and to show that, even though we cannot know the whole of the divine design and purpose, we are at least offered the possibility of discerning it in part and of realizing that it has to do with the raising of earth man's consciousness and the quality of his living, and particularly with his more widespread awakening to a greater understanding and recognition of his own true identity. It must be realized that God is effectively in physical form on earth to the extent that man consciously accepts his spiritual responsibility as a creator and his ego ceases to usurp that role. This has crucial implications for our more enlightened understanding of what is widely known as the Second Coming of Christ, to which there are many allusions in these pages. Whatever else may be implied by this teaching, there exists today a challenge to all who would be emissaries of light and peace to demonstrate in their thousands and in their hundreds of thousands the truth of *being* as the mainspring for the corporate outer expression which will effectively lead to establishing on earth the Kingdom of Love, Joy and Peace, filled with men, women and children rejoicing together in true brotherhood and in awareness of being first and foremost sons and daughters of a majestic *living* Universe and, as planetary citizens, holding a special responsibility and capacity for creating a world of hitherto unimagined splendour and glory. Since we speak of the manifestation of a new consciousness never yet corporately expressed upon the earth, such a world—notwithstanding brief glimpses such as are given in this book and in revealed insights given to many at this time—must far surpass man's highest aspirations and remain at present beyond the power of words to describe. But of one thing we may be sure. To the extent that we become aware of those powerfully creative energies working within our being— energies of light, love and wisdom, of joy and of peace; to the extent that we open up to let these indwelling energies do their transforming work within our hearts and minds and then radiate outwards, letting ourselves *be* the expression of the radiant qualities of Eternal Life, we *are* then, in this present moment, founders and creators of the New World.

Gövik, Särö,   Anthony Brooke
Sweden.   July, 1975.

Chapter One

There is nothing sensationally new in the statement that we live in a time of revelation. What is nowadays refreshing is an encouraging trend to abandon a tendency to confine the meaning of this word to other worldly implications and to awesome prohecies about the future of the planet.

It is of the nature of Life, whether we are speaking of the physical universe or of realms imperceptible to our five senses of which science is having increasingly to take note, to reveal itself to the listening, receptive and inquiring mind. Only when the human intellect falls away from a "listening" attitude and, assuming a self-sufficient pose in a state of broken communication with the Living Intelligence of which it is essentially a part, attempts to formulate its own ideas of what life is all about and how it can best be lived, does pain and suffering, confusion and conflict prevail upon the human scene.

The human condition is an undeniably painful one for the majority of people. Our overall condition is in some respects not unlike that of a teen-ager undergoing the pangs of adolescence while yet being unwilling to take the next conscious step towards the mature state, resisting Life's pressures to move with it along its unifying stream. To the extent that lessons are learned in proper timing and the listening attitude restored and adhered to, this painful separative experience, as in the case of the lost sheep rejoining its shepherd may, with heightened consciousness and growth in understanding, become a cause for special rejoicing. This possibility is always with us. For the bulk of humanity, however, and for the life of the planet as a whole this time of rejoicing has been overlong delayed and the pressure is now increasing upon human beings to pay more attention to Life's continuous revelation, ever available to open hearts and minds, of its unifying character, its laws and its design and purpose for man and for the universe.

There is therefore much that is offered in these pages which centres attention upon revelation and upon the restoration, as one might say, of the "missing link" with Life in its all embracing and indivisible wholeness. For only from the condition of the attuned state, the state of at-one-ment, can we speak meaningfully about achieving peace and human unity. For it then be-comes the externalisation of the beauty and harmony of Life living itself *through* us, *as* us. Authentic, qualitative living. Any attempt to achieve human unity through plans, programmes and pressuring policies designed by the separative human intellect of man, however well intended, will surely fail in the future as in the past.

Today, human concepts of every kind are being challenged as never before. Among the more deeply rooted of these is the absurd contention that "human nature can't be changed". This oft-repeated claim has long blinded man to his glorious potentialities and continues to hold many human beings in mental bondage. This statement of course is held to relate to human nature in the sense that we usually speak of it and if it were true there would be absolutely no hope for humanity. Man, however, through his encounters with experience upon experience, is a transitional being, attracted to ever higher states of manifestation and expression by the firmly held vision, which is his the moment he comes to accept it, of what he *essentially is* as embodying the seed of the infinite beauty and perfection of Life, of its Love, its Truth, its Wisdom, seeking ever to grow and unfold itself outwards from within him. If, as many believe, the truth of human beingness was demonstrated by the Master Jesus as "elder brother" within the human race, then the word "human" in the above quotation should read "sub-human" as being best descriptive of the condition which needs to be and is being, however slowly and painfully, transcended by the human race.

It is scarcely surprising that, with his confused concepts, man is urgently in need of a new vision of himself, of what he truly *is,* and the identity dilemma so widely spoken of and written about may be viewed as a healthy and encouraging sign of his searchings to discover the truth of it. Our formal educational institutions are of very little help to him in this matter : yet this is a question with which all our educational establishments might profitably be concerned. Indeed, at an educational seminar held under the auspices of the World Union International Centre, Pondicherry, India, a revolution in education was envisaged towards the aim of bringing forth "the essential universality secreted in the depths of the soul of the individual". Emphasis was laid upon the transformation of the individual rather than upon frantic endeavours to reform international institutions, though this of course is needed also. The individual, however, was viewed essentially as "the pivot of all evolutionary progress" and the seminar at which these views were expressed concluded that what is today most needed — and what many believe is in fact already though perhaps imperceptibly taking place — is a great mutation of the ideas which govern the world of the same order and magnitude as a biological mutation, one which would challenge world leaders to an extent that would induce them finally to abandon separative ways of thinking and move decisively beyond every consideration responsible for perpetuating the divisions among mankind.

These observations find an echo in a published statement made by U Thant, when Secretary General of the United Nations, in which he pointed out the tremendous possibilities for mankind to unite and determine its future course of development "if we stop being afraid of one another, harrying one another and if we together accept, welcome and prepare for the changes which must inevitably take place. If", added U Thant, "that means a change in human nature, well, it is high time to work at it."

Not only is a decision of the will involved here. That of course is indispensable. What is also needed is a widespread *empowerment* to change our ways of thinking and acting. St Paul was speaking of this problem when he told the Romans: "I can will what is right, but I cannot do it. For I do not the good I want, but the evil I do not want is what I do." Even if we do not always see it as a cut and dried choice between good and evil, most of us none the less need a greatly strengthened spirit to enable us to express and maintain the highly qualitative life which is deeply our heart's desire.

How is this to come about? Since, apart from a reformed will, strength of spirit seems to be the crucial factor, does it seem unreasonable to view this as a spiritual problem? Many of the world's leading thinkers and scientists seem to be in agreement with this way of viewing it.

The well known historian, Professor Arnold Toynbee, tracing the rise and fall of twenty one civilisations, shows how each in turn crashed on account of spiritual weakness, from failing to give sufficient expression to higher values within a civilisation overwhelmingly concerned with its emphasis upon material development and material power. From this he concludes that a spiritual change in the nature of man is vital if we are to make a breakthrough beyond this depressing repetitive cycle, a change which will be seen initially to be occurring within great numbers of individual human beings.

The noted biologist, Professor Julian Huxley, tells us that as an alternative to man's self-destruction by violence from the failure to transcend his present evolutionary level, there lies the conscious choice to evolve into a wholly new species, which will lift him beyond his animal tendencies and the brutal ways which have been so prominent a feature of his behavioural patterns.

The Indian sage and spiritual leader, Sri Aurobindo, in his *Life Divine* proffers a vision of what he terms the supramental power, which he sees bringing about a change in the consciousness of man that will lead to a reorganisation of the world towards the manifestation of its greater perfection.

Pierre Teilhard de Chardin, Catholic priest and scientist, writes about the coming "divinisation" of the world and what he calls the "christification" of man.

Although Truth is One it is, like most diamonds, many faceted. The world today teems with teachers and prophets, known and unknown, of every description and quality, one and all available to meet the needs of every sort and condition of man in his many and varied states and stages of search for an understanding of himself and of what is happening in his world and universe, as changes now come fast and thick both within him and in the life around him.

If the following pages are found helpful as a modest introductory guide to the nature of this crisis of transition, for man and for the planet, and provoke thought and further inquiry along lines and in areas judged by the

discriminating reader to be those best suited to his own pursuit of understanding, they will have served their purpose. What may need to be emphasised is
that it is no part of the purpose of these pages to advocate any particular
teacher or teachings to the reader. Life in and through all its forms in
each successive moment of our lives never fails to provide us with just those
outer experiences and "teachers" needed for our growth and learning. It is
only in those periods when, individually or corporately, we resist the
opportunity to grow and deepen in understanding that pressures build and
an "explosion" of some kind eventually takes place. We then have a special
opportunity of learning valuable lessons through the way the unifying pressure
works, even if the course of human history points to our having still much
to learn, corporately speaking, and learn quickly if we are to mitigate the
further pain and suffering that a continuing sense of division and separation
within the body of man must otherwise bring upon us.

There is no dearth of religious and spiritual movements and organisations
demonstrating or professing to demonstrate the way out of suffering,
pointing the way from division to unity, from war to peace and towards
joyous, creative and abundant living. While it would be foolish to deny
the apparent effectiveness of the forces of division and dissension operating
upon the planet, the most basic energy of all is the all powerful force of
unification, continually at work throughout the universe as an expression of
Life's ultimate requirement that all its parts should experience the joy and
peace of unity.

There has been reference to the concept of "christification" as indicating
a process taking place in our time. This concept may be viewed as being
relatable to the widely held expectation of what Christians call the Second
Coming — the return of Christ to Earth — which corresponds for followers
of other world religions to the coming of a World Teacher.

It is for each to arrive at his own understanding and conclusions as to
what all this portends. But since I have chosen to incorporate in these
pages information which moves right into this sensitive area, there is no
way properly to avoid the consequences of so doing and wholly to sidestep
a controversy which in our time, regarded by many as the end of an epoch, is
likely to become increasingly topical and made more so in the light of
the prophecy reported to have been made by Jesus Christ in regard to
the false rumours that would be current at the end of the age.

The activities of any religious or spiritual movement centred upon a
founder who is viewed as being related specifically to the Second Coming
concept will, therefore, inevitably provoke controversy. There may be other
such movements in the days ahead, but the storm is already gathering around a
movement with which I have been closely in touch in recent years and towards
which it seems appropriate publicly to clarify my own attitude. But first I
would like to say something further about the concept of "christification".

This concept, to which I admit to being attracted, implies to my understanding that we have entered an epoch in which, using Christian terminology, the seed of Christ, the God-seed if you will, is in process of flowering within humanity on a scale which now makes it possible by reason of the spreading conscious self-identification of an ever increasing number of individuals as true sons and daughters — *expressions* — of God, for humanity and the life of the planet to undergo what may be describable as a divine transformation or, using Pierre Teilhard de Chardin's graphic term, the *divinisation of the earth.* Humanity in fact is now to take responsibility consciously and joyously for bringing this transformation about. We are being called upon to accept the "mission" of acting both individually and corporately *as* Christ — the Son of God — and so to assume, at last responsibly, our inherited God-given dominion over the earth. This is not to deny that Christ may also reappear specifically in a single form but we may well have to revise many rigid and limited concepts about what the Second Coming means and possibly to accept it as a cosmic operation with many facets which is already taking place.

It is this possibility that lends special interest to the revelation, mission and movement of Sun Myung Moon of Korea. An electronic engineer in his earlier years, he is founder of the Holy Spirit Association for the Unification of World Christianity and of the International Cultural Foundation with its aims to confront scientists and scholars in various fields with the need to relate their activities to a universal standard of value for all mankind. The activities of this movement now reach into many countries, comprising businesses to support financially the work of the various foundations which have been brought into existence. The movement consists of highly dedicated and committed individuals and, notwithstanding its name, it attracts members from many different religions and draws to it those who have not previously been associated with any spiritual or religious movement at all.

One of its foremost challenges is the way its members come to view the person of its founder, who does not claim to avoid being controversial. At a meeting held in the eastern part of the United States on the occasion of his first visit to the U.S.A., a questioner bluntly asked him: "Are you Christ?" In reply Sun Myung Moon raised his hand and pointed to various members of the audience in turn, saying: "and so are *you. . .* and *you. . .* and you also, if you can accept it." On another occasion a translation of what he said in the Korean language was given as follows: "This is God's world and it has no boundaries. It is one. Your life is one of universal significance and I call upon you to share my mission. Be urgently concerned for the world and know, feel and act in accordance with the Divine Will. The purpose of the coming Lord is that some day all shall be like him — like Christ."

It is not my intention to enter into a discussion about the cosmological teachings of this movement, translated from the Korean revelation into a number of different English versions, except to say that it inherits certain clearly drawn battle lines about what is "good" and what is "evil" according to Christian dogma, together with much that is new and revolutionary in its interpretation of biblical passages. Bearing in mind the geographical position of its founder situated in southern Korea it is not perhaps altogether surprising that the movement takes an ideological stance in relation to communism.

It may well be that Christian dogma which so consistently stresses the struggle between two powers, the power of Good and the power of Evil, is in need of being brought into the light for thorough re-examination and possible transformation, together with every other concept to be found in the racial subconscious of man as we prepare to move with a resurrected and wholly unifying consciousness into a new age and a new understanding of Life.

Meanwhile for many of us there will be evils to fight and dragons to slay and organised movements to be expanded so that power may be mobilised to deal with these single and corporate evils more effectively. As happens in evangelistic movements, allegations of improper "pressuring" of members arise. Every movement, as with the individual members flowing in and out of it, has its own evolutionary development and challenges to be faced and overcome.

We each need to take our own stand in these great questions which are now before us and which are touched upon throughout this book. If we should have clear guide lines for ourselves in regard to what is "right" and "wrong"at any moment of our lives, in any situation or relationship, well and good; but we may need to be alert to the temptation to project our concepts upon others. It may well be nearer to the truth of things, whether consciously or unconsciously we are aware of it, that we are all participating in a vast process of learning and of ever continuing purification in which "rights" and "wrongs" may even change place for individuals according to their particular situation and the level of consciousness and understanding through which at any time they may find themselves moving. Only we ourselves, through inner listening, will know what is "right", and for those looking on from outside the words of the Master Jesus "Judge not that ye be not judged" may have a depth which is perhaps yet to be explored.

In the coming years our entire society and civilisation will be radically and increasingly challenged by the spiritual forces of transformation working both from invisible realms and through individuals and movements of every kind. According to our roles within society and our sense of identification shall we assume our responsibilities and take our stand. The movement which I have singled out will certainly not stand alone upon the field of controversy and others mentioned within these pages may well become equally controversial.

With this in mind, it may be wise to withhold judgment and unite our thinking and understanding with all the unifying tendencies we are able to perceive to be at work in individuals, in movements and in organisations of every kind. In this way we shall be making a valuable contribution to the realization of human unity.

Chapter Two

This is a time when, throughout the world, we are witnessing dramatic changes in the consciousness and nature of man, and when humanity in its evolution is in my conviction moving at an ever accelerating pace towards a cosmic breakthrough for which the whole of past human history has been, as it were, a preparation. There is no longer a recognizable frontier between the natural and the supernatural, even as there is no longer a frontier between matter and non-matter. All such boundaries are melting and merging before our very eyes. Scientists are already acknowledging a conception of matter which corresponds more nearly to a spiritual than to a material universe and will duly discover that matter and the physical are only different aspects of a single spiritual universe, divinely ordered, which has always been our true home, awaiting our awakening—or our re-awakening—to this truth.

Dr. J.B. Rhine, the eminent authority on extra-sensory perception, recently told an overflow audience in the Guildhall, London, that his discoveries compel a reclassification of the nature of man, and that materialist labels no longer apply to an organism capable of non-physical exchange. It is significant that Dr. Rhine calls attention to our need to face the fact "that the universe is such that these things can happen" and that no present-day conception of nature can account for what is now scientifically provable to be taking place in the realm of the mind. Indeed, it is noteworthy that these investigations have led to the establishment of a Foundation for Research on the Nature of Man and have already grown to the point where they involve international co-operation extending into Eastern Europe.

Although these disclosures might appear somewhat commonplace to mystics down the ages, it is none the less important and appropriate that these scientific initiatives should have an even more adventurous championship in the establishment of Spiritual Frontiers Fellowship. This body was incorporated by about 75 religious leaders and writers from all parts of the United States. Spiritual Frontiers Fellowship stresses the fact that man is a citizen both of the visible and of the invisible worlds, which interpenetrate one another, and puts forward a plea that all human experiences, including extra-sensory perception, clairvoyance, precognition and other related phenomena should be studied, without prejudice, for a better understanding of man. It may well be—and I personally hold it to be true—that for all of us in time these two worlds are destined to melt and merge and be perceived as one.

Primarily, it is a *spiritual* and an *evolutionary* crisis with which humanity is now confronted, and the nature of this crisis makes the present moment unique in the four billion years' history of our planet. Many people like to view evolution as something which takes place gently and gradually, but it is not always like this. Opinion today widely seems to veer between the view that human evolution may be halted or even terminated by a nuclear holocaust and the optimistic expectation that our universal nuclear crisis will somehow be met and overcome through enlightened political action linked with intensified educational campaigns, and finally the saving emergence of the reign of tolerance and reason, as man moves towards a better mutual understanding and the solution of the acute and complex problems which now beset him. It is true that for the first time in history man as a species has developed a capacity for total destruction, and the problem therefore humanly centres around the question, *how can man be prevailed upon and empowered to make the radical changes in thinking and living which are indispensable for his survival and for his evolution into a higher state of being?* Our crisis internationally is not unrelated to the fact that we comprise about 120 sovereign states, each claiming the right to make and wage war, while at the same time we have an ever-increasing proliferation of nuclear weapons. It needs no prophet to predict that with continuing world-wide fear and mistrust between nations and ideological groupings we are heading for some huge disaster.

In the course of the past few years I have been meeting and linking with quite small groups all over the world and with individuals who have been groping together to seek insights into what is going on around us; and I intend here to take a deep plunge into some conclusions which have been forced upon me. Even if I shall be making exceptional demands upon you, I shall hope at this point still to keep you with me.

If we are to grapple with the full significance of the events of our time, we shall need to find within ourselves a capacity to embrace what is at the core of all the world religions, bridge any gap which may seem to exist between religion and modern science, and at the same time keep a lifeline open to the thinking of sincere marxists. Is it possible for Christians to do this and yet remain true to Christ? An affirmative answer to this question can, I think, be found in the Jesuit scientist Pierre Teilhard de Chardin, whose life and work enshrines the highest expressions of both science and Christianity. It is therefore scarcely surprising to find among the many different groups mushrooming up in the world today a growing number of Teilhard de Chardin associations. Only if we can see Christ in cosmic terms can we, like Pierre Teilhard, see the entire cosmos in terms of Christ, and this breathtaking vision is one which coming events will make indispensable. Our Christianity needs not to be narrower than this.

We may be reminded that it was one of the earliest Fathers of the Christian Church, St. Augustine, who first introduced the Christocentric theme into human history. Some of you will recall his remarkable statement: "This which we now call the Christian religion existed among the ancients and was from the beginning of the human race until Christ himself came in the flesh, from which time the already existing true religion began to be called Christianity." In this cosmic age it seems natural to find humanity through every religious faith and expression being drawn ever closer to the Cosmic Christ, and to see the whole of creation moving to form the One Body of Christ, not as some vague mystical concept, but a real, even physical evolutionary process in which we are called consciously to participate. Man, says Pierre Teilhard, is evolution grown conscious of itself. The entire universe is the Cathedral of Christ.

Whether we realize it or not, the process of unification going on all around us is irreversible. The pressure of life itself is toward unity, and ever greater pressure is being exerted upon us to unite. Wars, racial conflicts and the periodic splitting up of social, religious, economic and territorial groupings which have come together may be viewed from the larger vision as reactions against this immense and growing pressure towards unity, somewhat after the manner of the seemingly receding waves on the shore as the water moves inexorably towards high tide.

New and living energies are flooding into our consciousness, and a new understanding is beginning to emerge. All over the world there is now a pouring out of these energies, these high frequency vibrations, upon us, and a welling up of them within us, and this is the source of modern revelation which confirms that God is speaking to man as urgently and as powerfully today as he has ever done in the past. Of course, there is the need to discriminate and sift the mass of material that is being channelled through the minds of those who are serving as conscious instruments to bring through to humanity the ideas that are to come to birth in our time: these are our prophets of the present day. But even if the purity of the channel may often be in question, it would be unreasonable to disregard the overwhelming accumulation of evidence directing our attention to events which are to take place in the skies and upon the earth. The core of a great many of these prophetic messages is one and the same, even though the instruments through which these messages come are not in physical contact or communication and often live continents apart.

Christians are inevitably beginning to ask themselves if all this has any bearing on the Parousia, or what is commonly called "The Second Coming." Three years ago I had no thought of this teaching in my mind, yet now I find it difficult to think of anything else. As is the case with many people today, this theme even impinges on my dreams, and I find as I move around the world that a great number of people of different faiths are expecting a new avatar or world saviour, while the Hopi tribe of North America are proclaiming that the Day of Purification by the Great Spirit is now at hand. They say this message is not only for Hopi Indians but for all people everywhere.

There are an estimated 900 million Christians in the world today, and surely it is the true vocation of the Christian Church as far as possible to prepare the peoples of the world for this event. All the signs are simultaneously in evidence as never before, with famines, epidemics and earthquakes since the beginning of the present century taking an ever-increasing toll of life. The great influenza epidemic after World War I, sweeping the face of the earth, took a greater toll than the war itself, and was responsible for the death of between 15 and 20 million persons. Although throughout all history there have been wars and rumours of wars, it was only with World War I that we began to have nation against nation, and kingdom against kingdom, with some 42 nations either actively or passively engaged before the Armistice. Since then, earthquakes, famines and floods have occurred with increasing frequency, an immense advance in knowledge has been accompanied by growing confusion as regards spiritual and ethical values; and serious crime has mounted so that it now outstrips the capacity of the authorities in many countries to deal with it. Along with this, there is taking place in our time an unprecedented revival of interest in spiritual matters, and new manifestations of the movement of the Holy Spirit which is by no means confined to the Pentecostal churches, and which is inevitably bridging by its impact denominational differences. With radio and television, to say nothing of Telstar, close communication links are being forged across the globe, and it can in our century for the first time be claimed that the Gospel is being preached throughout all the world.

It is when all these signs together are present that Christ Jesus says he will come again, and his frank and unequivocal reply to a direct question regarding the signs of his Coming Again is reported in three of the gospels. If we are called to pay heed to any of the sayings of our Lord, surely we should today pay close attention to these passages. For the Second Coming is the realization and completion of the Christian expectation, and even if many Christians seem unmindful of it, we are in fact called to anticipate this event and show our faith in the Second Coming every time we partake of the Holy Sacrament. Moreover, the wording of the references to this event in the New Testament is such that, despite ingenious and "reasonable" attempts to water down their full implication, it seems clear that these were intended to refer not merely to a spiritual event or condition, but also to an unmistakable physical happening. You will recall that at the time of the Ascension two men "in white apparel" appeared and said: "Men of Galilee, why stand there looking up into the sky? This Jesus, who has been taken away from you up to heaven, will come in the same way as you have seen him go." The invention of television, and the scientific possibility that even the sky itself may conceivably, by means of one of the belts surrounding the earth's atmosphere, be used as a giant television screen, invests the statement "every eye shall see him" with added plausibility. But we are to expect his appearance to be more physical than this.

It seems that something needs to be said about the understandable scepticism that widely exists in regard to what many people would hold to be a most unlikely happening. Yet only the fantastic is likely to be true at the cosmic level as Pierre Teilhard once remarked, and we can certainly appreciate how utterly incredible a prophecy of even some of the developments which have recently taken place in the world would have seemed to our ancestors living a mere two or three generations ago. The last word on the matter of his Coming Again was said by Christ Jesus himself, in his warning that everything would appear to be going along normally when *suddenly*, as lightning strikes from the east to the west, this great cosmic event would be upon us, and take a great many of us unprepared. We are told that we cannot know the day nor the hour, yet since revelation is continuous it would be foolhardy to disregard the intimations which are being given to man through the outpouring of the Spirit which is taking place in our time.

There are many striking examples that could be given of present-day dreams, visions and paranormal experiences which point to the imminence of great changes coming to our consciousness and our mode of life on earth. Many of them are indicative that human history as we have known it hitherto is coming to an abrupt end and is to give way to some wholly new beginning perhaps even in a new dimension of time and space. All that is taking place in terms of these world-wide intimations is in my understanding embraced by the Universal Link, which essentially has no geographical location and is the name given to a universal operation. It is not an organization or a teaching and its focus is upon *preparation* for the Day of Revelation. Preparation for this event is now deemed to be the only truly relevant consideration. A Christ-like archetypal figure is being seen in seemingly solid form in different parts of the world, appearing and disappearing. He seems to speak objectively and, giving his name as "Truth," states that he is appearing all over the world in different forms, according to the power of people to perceive him. He talks about being "intent on bringing My earth plane to realize My very presence by practical means best recognizable by man," and says that by Christmas, 1967, "I will have revealed myself to the universe through the medium of nuclear evolution." Many are to receive their own confirmation about this, and, it appears, are doing so. Commenting on the term "evolution", he states: "Modern evolution is but a directive from My Father, who governs all." He speaks about the "lifting of the veil which prevents complete Universal sight," and says: "there will be a speeding up of the Universal vibrations from which there will be many outward happenings to many." He says: "I mean the New Age by the Coming Again" and that "this refers to the New Vibration and Divine Energy that is feeding My Universe at this moment."

This is a continuing revelation and is being closely watched by the Churches' Fellowship for Psychical and Spiritual Studies. Emphasis is placed on the universal linkage which is now taking place throughout the world, and on the restoration or establishment of a Direct Link with the Divine.

It would be difficult for Christians not to relate these messages, unless they dismiss them altogether, to the doctrine of the Second Coming. It is also possible for non-Christians and those who hold agnostic views to link many of these messages with the way things seem to be moving in the world at this time, and conceivably with some widespread breakthrough beyond our present three-dimensional experience into a realm of truth which it has hitherto been impossible for us to experience due to the limitation of our five senses. These senses, as scientists are beginning to admit, give access only to a partial and therefore an essentially false understanding of the total realm in which we live.

It might well be asked whether the kind of happenings we have been discussing are considered in any way plausible by those concerned to look at these things from the scientific point of view. Since the nucleus of the atom relates specifically to the cohering force which holds everything in place from the tiniest atomic particle to the largest galaxy, it might be rash to claim that nothing dramatic could happen as man proceeds with his scientific experiments in nuclear evolution. And it is perhaps of some interest to report that agnostic scientists concerned with nuclear research are among those whose consciousness is today being impacted by experiences which are bringing them to an appreciation of the truth of spiritual reality. There would also seem to be some connecting link between what we have been saying and the following remarks of a government scientist who, drawing attention to the increase in sunspot activity and the abnormal behaviour of radio wave propagation, goes on to say: "I think our solar system is drifting through space on a collision course with a large body of matter, mostly hydrogen, in a very rarified state. I estimate this mass to be about 330 times that of our sun, and about 150,000 times the diameter of our solar system. Within this embryonic star there is bound to be quite a collection of cosmic debris, and if we are due to pass through the middle of it, we will be in for a pretty rough time. The fact that the sun will be gaining hydrogen during its passage will result in increased solar activity, with accompanying increase in temperature and surface disturbances, earthquakes and a general change in topography. I think we are just now entering the outer fringes of this cosmic mass. This speculation," he concludes, "seems to be in line with predictions contained in the Holy Bible, current scientific observations throughout the world, and my own observations."

If we accept the view that the peoples of this planet are to be given the opportunity of making an evolutionary breakthrough into a new and higher condition, transcending the human condition as we have known it from the beginning of recorded history, then I think we shall find the wording of the following message of extraordinary interest and relevance. The message in question was dictated by "Truth" during one of his appearances in 1961:

"A major world conflict will herald the last stage of the Universal progress. In the meantime general world conditions will show evidence of a leading up to the introduction of a nuclear device that will bring about the final human level episode. The major conflict I speak of will be between nations and it will be most sudden. A war will start in Asia and spread to the Western World. A human press button device will be used and, simultaneously with the pressing of the button, instead of disaster, the Universal Revelation will occur."

I am sure none of you will fail to have noted that, provided this climax of history is devoutly to be hoped for and in no way feared, then the use of the terms "Universal progress" and "final human level episode" seems justified. In fact, in no other context would this extraordinary choice of words make sense.

This is not of course to justify the prophesied means by which the ending of the present state of affairs is to be brought about, any more than one would seek to justify Judas' betrayal of Christ Jesus as a desirable pattern for human conduct on the ground that it led on to the Resurrection and the demonstration that has ever since been present among us in the power of the living and healing Christ. This message may, however, serve to remind us that, although as Christians we are pledged to be peacemakers and to engage in peacemaking according to our insights and understanding of what this may mean in the light of our differing circumstances and opportunities, it will always till the end of time be a matter of dealing as with the festering boils of a man sick unto death, whose condition may be eased but not cured. Enduring world peace will come, and can come only with the Return of Christ. This is to be both an outer manifestation of Love-Power in form, and an inner realization of Grace—the Christ consciousness within.

In the world as it is there will always be tribulation and wars, but from the scriptures and from modern revelation we do know one thing. The world as we now experience it is coming to an end. Those of us who pray for God's Kingdom to come and for his Will to be done on earth ought not to be surprised when at last we find this age-long prayer being answered in our time. The final unification will be the uniting of the heavenly and earthly states and the overcoming of death here on earth. It may be an awe-filled moment as this event falls upon us: yet we shall hold fast to Christ and know that all is well, and now is the time for us to expect it and prepare for it.

"First of all," writes St. Peter according to a modern translation, "you must realize that in the last days mockers will undoubtedly come and they will say: 'What has happened to his promised Coming? Since the first Christians passed away everything remains exactly as it was since the beginning of creation!' Yet it remains true that the Day of the Lord will come as suddenly and unexpectedly as a thief in the night. In that day the heavens will disappear in a terrific tearing blast, the very elements will disintegrate in heat and the earth and all that is in it will be burnt up to nothing... True, this day will mean that the heavens will disappear in fire and the elements disintegrate in fearful heat, but our hopes are set not on these but on the new heavens and the new earth which he has promised us and in which nothing but good shall live." This passage has been regarded by many people as a remarkable vision of a nuclear holocaust, and were it not for the assurance of Divine intervention and the infusion into man's consciousness of these new divine love energies of which we have been speaking, human ignorance and our absence of patience and control over our own forces—all stemming from a lack of compassionate love—could well result in St. Peter's prophecy being fulfilled. The point I wish to make is that these end-time prophecies from the scriptures are now being re-examined and reinterpreted in the light of modern revelation coming to man all over the world, while circumstantial evidence very strongly suggests the time in question is now upon us.

This chapter would be incomplete without a mention of telepathic messages purporting to be coming from the inhabitants of other planets, many of them beyond our solar system, which reflect an apprehension that we may by some foolhardy act set fire to the earth's outer atmosphere, which consists largely of helium. These messages are being received in different parts of the world and are generally accompanied by intimations to the effect that our activities have long been observed by these friendly and highly evolved visitors from outer space, who are ready to welcome us into their interplanetary brotherhood the moment we show signs of becoming a little more civilized. In fact, their purpose in coming is to help their brother man on planet Earth as the New Age dawns. The principal governments of the world know about these matters, but are at present somewhat confused. Clearly nothing is more likely to result in a dramatic transformation almost overnight of the worldwide ordering of affairs on earth than the enforced admission by governments that government as we know it, including the entire gamut of our national self-defence systems, is outdated. Many things are being kept from the peoples of the world which they need to know at this time, but all doubts will soon be removed as our visitors from outer space begin to show themselves in greater numbers all over the world.

Some of you may be wondering if it is a mere coincidence that I have mentioned this somewhat controversial subject in the same breath, as it were, with the equally controversial subject of the Second Coming. It may prove true, and I think it will, that there is a very close connection between the two. It is certainly interesting that reports are pouring in of strange appearances and disappearances of entities who speak of being able to raise and lower at will the frequencies of the atomic particles of which their bodies are composed, so that they are able to appear in seemingly solid form and then disappear from sight. This seems to be a step further along the line of conscious evolution than we have attained to at present, but they claim also to be the children of the same Creator and so regard us as their brothers. As we re-read our bibles, we may begin to wonder if such beings have not sometimes appeared to man in the guise of angels. After all, the original meaning of the Greek word for angel is simply "messenger," and the message they are bringing to mankind today is broadly to the effect that we should look to the skies and keep watch; that we should hold fast to the roots of our faith and mend our ways. We are also clearly being told that we are soon to enter a new dimensional state, and that we are to expect some confusion and suffering as individually and in groups all over the world these new divine energies now being released upon the earth and into our consciousness begin to take effect upon us, and transform and transmute us into our new conditions of experience and aware- ness. Whether we like it or not, want it or not, we are to become changed beings through the love and power of God, so that we may be fit to live in the new heaven on earth which has been promised us.

It is our ignorance of what is taking place, and our resistance to this process and gift of transformation, which will bring mankind a measure of suffering and confusion. We therefore need urgently to meet in small groups to discuss these things, and above all to pray for insight into the truth of them and that our power of discernment may be sharpened. Only as we begin to understand the immensity of what is happening in our time shall we learn to be equipped to link effectively with this cosmic event and at the same time, in freedom from the confusion that will be taking place around us, shall we with God's grace be enabled and empowered to help others through the tur- moil and stress of the coming days.

Speaking evolutionarily, humanity is in the chrysalis stage. We are soon to emerge into as different a life as does the dragonfly emerging from its sheath: thenceforth we shall enter the realm of direct intuitive perception, with our lost link with the Divine at last restored. Meanwhile we are living through the death agony of the old order and are being simultaneously torn by death throes and birth pangs in which all our vital forces are involved.

In the same way as through the whole of physical creation there flows a single energy linking atoms together as it does molecules and cells, this same unifying force manifesting through mankind and directing us toward unity and brotherhood is given the name of *love.* What an unprecedented leap for- ward in the quality and intensity of our love is needed before we can make the evolutionary breakthrough now required of us in living consciousness! We shall succeed only as we come to realize that our uninspired efforts, though they be humanly of the best, are leading us towards irrevocable disaster. What- ever the pride of man may tell him, we do desperately need help. Events are soon to drive us in our millions to call upon God, and then will the end come. The promise of the ages will be fulfilled as Christ with his heavenly hosts manifests with power and glory in our midst to usher in the rule of love and truth on earth.

How many of us are *expecting* this Coming Light?

Are These the Signs?

Chapter Three

In my continuous travels in many lands it has become most evident to me that an ever increasing number of individuals both within the churches and outside them are having experiences of a mystical and psychical nature and are receiving spiritual gifts, especially the gifts of healing and glossolalia—or speaking in tongues—to an extent which must incline thoughtful people to search for some overall meaning to these apparently worldwide manifestations.

I would like to share with you some of my recent experiences in the U.S.A. and the investigations I have been making, first into a remarkable type of psychic or etheric surgery; secondly into a case of alleged translation; and in conclusion a story which relates to the increasing number of reports we have been reading and hearing about "flying saucers", a subject which I think can no longer be lightly dismissed or underestimated in the context of the mighty events which are coming to mankind at this time.

Some time ago I paid an eight day visit to the home of a highly dedi-cated couple, the Rev. William C. Brown and his delightful wife, Nancy. They live in Toccoa, Georgia, about 100 miles north-east of Atlanta. I had heard reports of Mr. Brown's splendid work while I was in California, and through an exchange of correspondence a date was set for me to undergo a full etheric diagnosis and to be operated upon in any way that might prove necessary or desirable. It was agreed that the best way of investigating this type of healing was to submit to a personal experience of it, and I want to tell you in quite precise terms what takes place.

The patient is required to arrive at the Centre at least one day before he is due to undergo examination by the etheric doctors. No solid food is taken after breakfast on the day of the examination and the patient is required to go to his room and lie down from 11 a.m. until he is called into the surgery at 2 p.m. Here I must tell you that available to Mr. Brown in the realms of spirit is a team of 28 specialists, who claim to have been embodied as doctors and surgeons on the Earth plane and to be still concerned to perfect their skills by continuing in the service of suffering humanity as the means of expressing their dedication to God. The entire affair is conducted in a reverent atmos-phere. As the patient enters the surgery he finds himself listening to sacred music, and after a few minutes quiet Mr. Brown invites all who may be present to join in the saying of the Lord's Prayer. This is followed by a prayer asking that only the highest and best spiritual forces be attracted. Mr. Brown then goes into a trance and after a few moments his head is seen to fall forward between his knees. This is the moment when Mr. Brown leaves his body. When his body reassumes an upright position in the chair another entity with a distinctive speech and personality seems to have taken control of it. This entity gives his name as Dr. John Geoffrey Spaulding, who speaks with a pronounced English accent. After a few words of greeting he in turn gives way to another entity possessing an equally distinctive personality, who gives his name as Dr. John Murphy. Dr. Murphy is the diagnostician of the team; he has a strong sense of humour and speaks with an Irish inflection. The team includes heart specialists, orthopaedic specialists and neurological specialists, and according to the nature of the diagnosis given by Dr. Murphy an appropriate specialist takes control and performs the operation.

For those who do not yet have etheric vision—of which I am one—the operation is a somewhat strange affair. The hands which are normally regarded as belonging to the Rev. William Brown are seen to be making a series of rapid and precise movements a few inches above the body of the patient lying upon the operating table. This may continue for 15 or 20 minutes and then, after another specialist has taken over, a similar series of movements is seen to take place over another portion of the patient's anatomy. Some of these gestures, however, are clearly recognizable, such as the taking of invisible surgical instruments from invisible trays or from invisible nurses and helpers (I was politely yet sharply told on one occasion to get out of the way of the trays!); the administering of etheric injections and the making of invisible incisions on the etheric body. (At this point I might add for the benefit of those who are not too well acquainted with these matters that the etheric body is in all respects an exact counterpart of the physical form which it occupies, every organ, every nerve, bone and tissue precisely duplicated but in a finer density.) The principle behind etheric surgery is that, the etheric body being more basic than the physical, every adjustment made to the etheric body is in time—and the time factor varies—reflected in the physical counterpart, even as damage done to the physical body is reflected back into the etheric counterpart.

In order to make real to you the remarkable work performed through the Rev. William Brown I should like in conclusion to tell you about the operations performed upon Dr. A, who was staying at the Centre while I was there and whose operations on two successive days I was privileged to witness. Of my own operation I can say little—and perhaps this is just as well. Most of the time I was lying flat on my stomach and could see scarcely anything which took place.

Dr. A's story, however, is one which I would like to give in some detail, because his condition required the attention of three different surgeons and was as serious a case as any likely to be found within or outside any hospital.

Dr. A is 54 years old. He is a chiropractor. In August of 1965 he began to experience pain in his lower back and prostate and in September he went to a Chicago clinic for a complete medical check-up. X-rays and other tests revealed a condition of cancer in the pelvic girdle. The prostate was tender and swollen and he was told that his condition "could be cancerous." He went to another clinic for a re-check and his condition was in every respect confirmed. His suffering in the back and prostate gradually increased and he began to develop other disagreeable symptoms. In October and November the condition slowly spread to the lower rib cage and his pain was intensified until in December it became excruciating. He then developed a bony tumour in the head, which was perceptible both to sight and touch. The inflammation spread to his chest and in January, 1966, his feet began swelling. He went for another check-up in a third clinic and by this time he was suffering from high fever and profuse perspiration. At the end of 17 days spent in this clinic he went home because nothing more could be done for him. By this time he was convinced he had cancer and he continued with laetrile treatment at home. His wife had earlier read an article written by the Rev. William Brown and published in an issue of the Cosmic Star, a Californian psychic publication, and had exchanged correspondence with him. The weather at that time, however, was extremely bad and for other reasons, too, Dr. A felt disinclined to undertake the long journey from Colorado. Finally, however, as he told me himself, he was "psychologically ready" to visit the Rev. Brown, and the date for his examination by the etheric specialists was set for 26th April.

When Dr. John Murphy took over the Rev. William Brown's body to make the initial diagnosis, he asked without touching the patient's body that the following adjustments should be made by a chiropractor six weeks hence:

3rd, 4th and 5th cervicals out to the right 1¼ centimetres.
4th, 5th and 6th dorsals out to the right 3 centimetres.
2nd lumbar out to the right 1¾ centimetres.
3rd lumbar out to the left 1½ centimetres.
Coccyx inverted and hooked to the right.

Himself a chiropractor, Dr. A realized that such a diagnosis could not normally be made with such detailed precision without the assistance of X-rays and a centimetre ruler.

As regards Dr. A's more serious condition, Dr. Murphy made the following diagnosis and a series of operations were performed accordingly:

Tumour in the left frontal lobe of the brain.
Palpitation and regurgitation in the right ventricle of the heart, involving calcium deposits in the mitral and tricuspid valves.
Sarcoma involving transverse, descending and ascending colons, and prostate gland.
Massive sarcoma in 11th and 12th ribs and throughout the pelvis. Pelvic sockets replaced with bone graft from right tibia.
2 cysts behind the pancreas. 6 stones in the gall bladder.

Before the operation on the brain tumour was done, Mrs. Brown, Mrs. A and myself were invited to feel it, which we all did in turn. After the etheric operation the tumour seemed, when re-examined, immediately to have been dissolved, as the patient himself confirmed. The three of us, and the patient himself, were also invited to check by means of a stethoscope the palpitation and regurgitation of the heart. We each noted the unmistakable periodic swishing sound. After the etheric operation on the heart, which took about 17 minutes, but which if carried out physically might have taken around three hours, the heart was found, according to the stethoscope, to have been immediately freed from its palpitation and from all irregularity. The Rev. Brown later admitted that it was unusual for the effect of an etheric adjustment of such a serious nature to take effect so quickly in the physical body.

It is, I think, significant to note that Mrs. A, the patient's wife, had worked in the Medical Branch of the Women's Army Corps during World War II, as a surgical technician. She had witnessed innumerable operations and testified to us all that the quick and deft movements of the hands when operating were exquisite to watch, and although she does not possess etheric sight she could recognize without any difficulty and with heartfelt admiration the precision and quality of the surgical work that was being done.

It only remains for me to add that the Rev. William Brown has no naturally acquired skills and no professionally acquired medical knowledge. In the war he served in the Merchant Marines: his hobby is flying. He is now a Minister of Philosophy. He makes no claims of any kind and is himself the essence of humility in regard to the work done through him. An increasing number of grateful patients exist to tell their story in letters they have written to him. Evidence also exists in the form of X-rays and cardiograms, taken before and after operations. If anyone should wish to inquire further about the Rev. William Brown's work, inquiries should be sent to R.R.1, Box 64-E, Collier Road, Toccoa, Georgia 30577, and stamps would be appreciated for reply.

Science today is showing that living cells have within them the elements of continuous life, and in psychic circles it is being repeatedly proclaimed that the atomic structure of our physical bodies is under constant bombardment by high frequency energies which are stimulating all cell life on this planet. We are being told through psychic intimation that this is resulting in the gradual replacement of our present physical bodies by bodies of a lighter density, and that much of our mental confusion and physical discomfort at this time is due to the varying degrees of resistance to this pressure of evolutionary change and transformation which we consciously or unconsciously manifest. It is contended in these circles that an immense cosmic operation is taking place, over which we virtually have no control whatever apart from a capacity to be in varying degrees responsive or resistant to it. Although scientifically-minded individuals might tend to dispute this contention, the eminent scientist Sir Arthur Eddington rather neatly expressed this condition when he said on one occasion: "Something unknown is doing we don't know what." Dr. Albert Einstein was a little more articulate when he said: "Anyone who pursues physics far enough is eventually forced into metaphysics because if we examine matter closely enough it disappears and we find nothing but a frequency of vibration." It may well eventuate that this seemingly ever-accelerating and all-pervasive frequency of vibration will compel our attention in the time ahead, when great changes are to take place in the consciousness of man and in the shape of terrestrial affairs. The greatest challenge to all of us in this time will involve our ability to maintain an inward calm and positive attitude as these developments take place within and around us.

I would like now to turn to the case of Miss Annalee Skarin, about whom some of you will have heard in connection with her authorship of the books "Ye are Gods," "To God the Glory," "The Temple of God" and other inspiring works. Her most recent book, "Man Triumphant," has just come out. Some of you may also have heard reports which are current that from time to time she appears and disappears in different localities in a quite mysterious way. She is believed by many people to have translated from this planet and more specifically from Salt Lake City, Utah, in June, 1952.

After hearing these reports I decided to visit Salt Lake City in the hope of meeting with some of the individuals who knew her well at the time of her alleged translation.

Annalee Skarin was at one time a member of the Mormon Church or, to give it its full appellation, of The Church of Jesus Christ of Latter Day Saints, and the publication of her first book "Ye are Gods" aroused the opposition of her Church, which forthwith excommunicated her. I was fortunately able to meet Apostle Mark E. Peterson, of the Council of Twelve of the Mormon Church, who was personally concerned in the circumstances of Miss Skarin's excommunication. Objections were raised at the time on the ground that Miss Skarin "places herself in the position of a revelator or prophetess, transmitting revelations by means of her books," and that this was "a contradiction of the order established by the Lord himself, who says that the President of the Church of Jesus Christ of Latter Day Saints is to be the one and only revelator for the Chruch." It was also held that her books were filled with false doctrine and that her teachings were widely at variance with the scriptures "which are the legitimate revelations of the Lord." Apostle Mark Peterson says that Miss Skarin is anti-Christ in that her teachings tend to nullify the atonement of Jesus Christ in her claim "that there shall be no more death, that death is unnecessary and that we ourselves can overcome and avoid death." According to Apostle Peterson it was a question of deciding "whether the doctrines of the Church are true or whether Miss Skarin's doctrines are true." In our conversation together Apostle Peterson, who received me most courteously, remarked that we were living in a time of false prophets, and when I questioned him on this subject he affirmed that according to his understanding no true modern prophet could be found outside the presidency of the Mormon Church. He held Miss Skarin to be "untruthful" and not to be in sound mental health.

During the 36 hours I was able to spend in Salt Lake City I was most fortunate in making four other significant contacts relating to this case. A bookseller, Mr. Eugene Wilson, who at one time enjoyed close acquaintance with Miss Skarin, told me that she had required him to distribute, free of charge, more than 500 copies of her first book. He described her as charming and "very sane," possessing a keen sense of humour and emanating what he could only define as a high spiritual quality. He expressed himself to be shocked by the attitude adopted by the Mormon Church and he seemed to imply that in his opinion Miss Skarin's writings—and he had read all her books —pointed rather to a fulfilment of the teachings of Jesus Christ in regard to the subject of death than to a contradiction of them. The barber who cut my hair surprisingly produced an album containing one of the finest collections of flying saucer pictures I have yet seen, and when I gingerly raised the subject of Miss Skarin he told me that he was actually present when the order of excommunication was publicly read out and before I left his shop he produced from an adjoining room a mass of correspondence containing copies of letters exchanged between Miss Skarin and some of those who looked to her for spiritual enlightenment. From this correspondence I copied out the following sentence from a letter dated 7th June, 1951: "All I am trying to do is to teach mankind that it is possible for every child of God to be so in tune with him and his Holy Spirit that they can be directed in all that they do—in all that they say—and that their lives can become a melody of living glory as they learn to abide completely and fully in his Holy Spirit. It is such a breathtaking glory every moment of every day that it is almost unspeakable in its power."

Of all my contacts perhaps the two most significant, apart from my meeting at the Mormon Church, took place with Miss Skarin's lawyer, who had known her since she was a child, and the lady, now elderly, in whose house the alleged translation took place in June, 1952. In order to respect their desire for anonymity I shall refer to them as Mr. G and Mrs. B. Both Mr. G and Mrs. B accept the translation as a fact and have no doubt about it at all. I had two long talks with Mr. G on my two evenings in Salt Lake City and there can be no question that he was intimately acquainted with Miss Skarin, whom he knew as a child, as also was Mrs. B, in whose house she stayed while living in Salt Lake City. Mr. G testified to her exceptionally high spiritual sensibility and unquestionable integrity and he told me he wound up her affairs at the time of her translation and she no longer has any personal worldly affairs though reports continue to circulate in regard to ways in which she still serves mankind as she takes up her body and leaves it again at will.

Mr. G pointed out to me that Miss Skarin would not want attention drawn to her personality, and yet it is impossible to speak of this subject without appearing to do this. Miss Skarin maintains in her writings that man has embryonic divinity within himself; that every minute brain cell of man's being can respond to Love, and take on the properties of Life and Light and Love; that every organ, cell, nerve, tissue and fibre of man's being can become spiritualized and transmuted, and that the experience of translation is not just for the few. It is intended for all. Yet, she insists, we should not have our minds fixed on translation but on unceasing prayer, praise and thanksgiving to God which, intensively engaged in, must lead to this result. Love, which is carried on the wings of Light, is to become active in every cell of man's being and given out *in strength.* "I want you," writes Miss Skarin in a letter to one of her circle, "to pray night and day every waking moment of your life for the gift of perfect, divine, Christ-like love." The emphasis is always on love, not on translation. Yet I feel I can only complete this account with the following remarkable story related to me by Mrs. B.

On the morning of 16th June, 1952, Miss Skarin intimated to Mrs. B that it had been revealed to her the previous night that, as she put it, "the angels might be coming" for her quite soon and during the day she left instructions that in the event of this happening all her books and personal effects should be sent to her daughter. Early the following morning Mrs. B awakened suddenly at 1.10 a.m. and went straight into Miss Skarin's room to find her gone, with her dentures on a table beside the bed and all her clothes left in the room. A strong yet delicate scent filled the entire house, and it was in fact this strong aroma which had awakened Mrs. B from her sleep. On the evening of the 17th June, around 10.30 p.m., when Mrs. B was sitting in the living room with her grown-up son and her two daughters, Miss Skarin entered the house wearing a plain blue dress, with her hair seemingly rather dishevelled and her legs covered with dust. She immediately spoke and asked: "Do you believe I have translated?" Mrs. B and the members of her family replied at once in the affirmative, whereupon Miss Skarin invoked blessings upon them at the same time praising God for their faith. While doing this, according to Mrs. B and her family, who all testify to the same story, Miss Skarin was transformed before their eyes into a shining being with white raiment. Mrs. B noted that the transformed Annalee Skarin evidently displayed her new and gleaming teeth and her hair shone with a golden light. She later disappeared from their sight.

We are today in the time of the re-establishment of direct contact with God and many wonderful things are taking place which test our faith and the tendency, however understandable it may be, to depend overmuch on the evidence of our five physical senses as if they were the yardstick for what alone may be regarded as true and real. In spite of the great knowledge modern science has brought us, we are surely glimpsing life imperfectly and incompletely so long as we remain slaves to what is called the scientific method and to this alone. There are times when we need to place a greater trust in our own direct intuitive perceptions, especially when we are dealing with matters which escape the measurements of science as we know it today.

To conclude this chapter I want to speak about the subject of "flying saucers" and to tell you something about the work and experience of Dr. Daniel Fry, Ph.D. and of their implications for our time.

The story of Dr. Fry illustrates in an outstanding way the impact made on an individual's life by his contact with intelligences from outer space. Dr. Fry, whose integrity and humility are in my view beyond question, insists that when an individual is granted an extraordinary experience he must be mindful of the responsibility that goes with it and also of the fact that every conceivable kind of experience has been happening to individual men and women since time began and the experience itself is unimportant compared with the supreme importance of what is made of it and of what the race of man as a whole can be prevailed upon to learn from it—those with hearts and minds that are open.

Dr. Fry was once employed by Aerojet General Corporation of White Sands Proving Grounds, New Mexico, where he was in charge of the installation of instruments for missile control and guidance. He developed a number of parts for the guidance system of the Atlas missile while holding the position of Vice-President in Charge of Research at Crescent Engineering and Research Company of California. He has also been employed by the California Institute of Technology as a consultant. He is the author of several books including "White Sands Incident" and "Atoms, Galaxies and Understanding."

During his period of service at White Sands Proving Grounds, Dr. Fry met with an experience about which he felt able to say nothing for two years, because he knew his story was unlikely to be believed. The incident in question occurred in July, 1950, when a space craft controlled from outside the earth's atmosphere landed near Dr. Fry and took him to New York and back in 25 minutes. During this time Dr. Fry was in continuous telepathic contact with an outer space being who said he might be identified by the name "Alan" and with whom a long conversation took place on scientific and philosophical matters. The whole story is told in "White Sands Incident," which can be obtained from Dr. Daniel Fry, P.O. Box 322, Merlin, Oregon (U.S.A.). As the result of the impact of this experience upon him, Dr. Fry's entire life has been changed and he has become Founder and National President of a movement called Understanding, Inc.—an international, non-profit organization dedicated to bringing about a greater degree of understanding among all of the people of this planet and preparing them for their eventual inevitable meetings with other beings in space. This movement is spreading widely throughout the U.S.A. and also to other countries, and I personally intend to do what I can to help to further its splendid aims.

As the result of what he has learned from his own personal experience Dr. Fry thinks it possible that extra-terrestrials may have an electronic device capable of modulating the auditory nerve currents in such a way that speech may be heard by us although no-one is speaking within the range of our hearing; or that they may even have discovered a way of modulating our nerve currents or brain waves directly without the need of intervening electronic devices. He points out that the ear is not essential for hearing and neither is sound, and that it is open to any electronic engineer to set up a device whereby the human body as a whole may become a radio receiving set with the nerves carrying the modulated current, which will be heard as sound and interpreted as speech. Dr. Fry also points out that there are many ways in which it might be possible for races technologically ahead of us to learn our languages. They would, for example, be able to monitor our television broadcasts and by having picture and sound constantly together they would learn the way a child does. In communicating with Dr. Fry Alan used the English language and to some extent the American idiom, although words were sometimes put together in a way we would not place them ourselves, and in the midst of a precise scientific statement a slang word would creep in.

It seems that Alan gave an interesting analysis of our present condition on Earth and claimed that our brothers in outer space had been visiting and studying Earth for a great many years with a view to determining the basic adaptability of the Earth race, particularly their ability to adapt their minds quickly and calmly to conceptions which are completely foreign to our customary modes of thought. Previous expeditions, it appears, met with almost total failure in this respect, but now there are minds sufficiently receptive to enable help to be given. I have found in my travels that the core of the messages from outer space, coming through sensitives in different parts of the world, comprises a combined warning in relation to our nuclear experimentation and an offer to communicate to us more advanced findings in the medical and scientific fields as soon as men of Earth show a greater readiness to listen. Alan has something rather pertinent to say in this respect. "Your Science," he says, "is attempting to make one lower limb take the place of the entire tree of knowledge with the result that your Science has become greatly over-complicated. What you define as E.S.P. is not 'extra-sensory' at all. It is just as much a part of the body's normal perception equipment as any other of the senses, except that it has been used so little by your people that it is still in a rudimentary state of development. Some of your animals and many of your insects have developed this sense to a higher degree than your people. There are three types of Science necessary for the proper evolution of mankind: Spiritual Science, Social Science and the Physical or Material Science. The difference between man and the animals is that the animal, having no Spiritual or Social Science—except in a very rudimentary form in certain insects such as the ant and the bee—has never developed a Material Science.

Mankind from the beginning sensed the fact that there is a Superior Power and Intelligence pervading and controlling all nature and, whether regarding it with fear and resentment or reverence and love, he has always had the desire to learn more of the nature of this Power. The realization quickly dawned that man could improve the conditions of his life only by co-operation. The superstructure of Material Science, being constantly stimulated by ever-increasing needs and desires of the body, has rushed ahead in the last half century at a rate which is always accelerating, leaving the Spiritual and Social Sciences far behind. So the true foundation is scarcely any longer able to support the massive material superstructure which must collapse upon it. Humanity is being threatened by its own creations simply because the Spiritual and Social Sciences have not progressed far enough to enable them to determine the uses to which their creations shall be put."

At this juncture I feel it might be helpful to link back with Dr. Fry's contention, with which I find myself in total agreement, that more important by far than the actual experiences which may come to any individual is our recognition of the fact that we live unceasingly in the midst of life of every conceivable description, and there is a task to be done, to probe deeply into these things and communicate our insights and understanding about them as widely as possible throughout the world. It is of course easier to resist and deny any truth that may lie in the matters we have touched upon here than to pay attention to them and open our minds to the immense possibilities here held out to us.

It would not personally surprise me if we were quite soon brought to view flying saucers as an important link between the spiritual and the material worlds and as a significant means to help us towards an understanding of the spiritual and universal oneness of all creation. It is interesting, I think, to re-call what Lenin is reported to have said to Mr. H.G. Wells, the eminent novelist, historian and writer of science fiction, when these two men met in the year 1920:

> "All human conceptions are on the scale of our planet. They are based on the pretension that the technical potential, although it will develop, will never exceed the terrestrial limit. If we succeed in establishing inter-planetary communications, all our philosophi-cal, moral and social views will have to be revised. In this case the technical potential, become limitless, would impose the end of the rule of violence as a means and method of progress."

From now onwards we shall witness and participate in the most tremen-dous events of all human history. Although we must continue to live our lives in the light of our own individual understanding, I do believe that in the time ahead we shall find ourselves freely abandoning the trivialities and unessentials of our living to prepare and fortify ourselves mentally and spiritually for great cosmic experiences which may come to us individually and collectively at any time. I believe that we are moving into a wondrous age and that many of us will experience travel at the speed of thought. I believe also that there is a most relevant truth in the scriptural reference in the Book of Isaiah, chapter 30, verses 20 and 21, which read: "And though the Lord give you the bread of adversity, and the water of affliction, yet shall not thy teachers be removed into a corner any more, but thine eyes shall see thy teachers; and thine ears shall hear a word behind thee, saying, this is the way, walk ye in it, when ye turn to the right hand, and when ye turn to the left." And I believe also in the imminence of St. Peter's vision (2 Peter, chapter 3, verse 10) of the elements melting with a fervent heat and the heavens passing away with a great noise. In this respect I share the Rev. Billy Graham's inspired insight given in his book, "World Aflame," that this climax which is coming will not be destruction but transformation. We know indeed that all elements can be changed by heat and this could well be the heat generated by the separation of the proton and neutron in the nucleus of the atom, which would release the tremendous heat energy in nature and by which this long promised cosmic event resulting in "a new heaven and a new earth" might well be brought about. It might in some cases lead to our being changed "in the twinkling of an eye."

As Jeremiah so beautifully expresses it: "And they shall teach no more every man his neighbour and every man his brother, saying 'Know the Lord,' for they shall all know Me, from the least of them to the greatest of them, saith the Lord." I believe we are all to know God by the power we are going to receive and that this will be less a "divine intervention" (though many may experience it as such) than the perfectly natural action of an ever-existent law involving the introduction of cosmic energy into the very atomic structure of all material objects and into the smallest atomic elements of our very beings.

The cosmic operation now upon us, in which all are called to participate, heralds unprecedented breakthroughs in understanding, which are to lead us through the morass and darkness of our present time into the emergence of an overall heightened spiritual awareness. In this expanded consciousness, which all are offered, we shall become cognizant of our universal link in love with the entirety of God's living creation throughout all the universes. If this may seem a mind-shattering vision, let us remain in no illusion about the cosmic character of the events which lie at hand. The choice indeed lies between the shattering of outdated mental concepts, which have lost their meaning in the conditions of our present hour, and their transformation and expansion so as to enable our minds more truly to attune to pre-existing yet newly emerging truths.

In the light of this heightening consciousness, which coming events are dramatically to intensify throughout the human race, we shall find ourselves becoming free from the selfish and self-defensive attitudes which for ages past have been binding us in chains and blocking our forward path to unity. We are on the threshold of being moved swiftly and unfailingly into attitudes and qualities of living more truly consistent with the fact that under One Divine Creator we are in very truth members of a single brotherhood of man and of one essentially indivisible human race. No longer, through unconscious automatic living, can we continue our lives on earth, nor even by more conscious and well-intentioned yet perhaps *uninspired* activity on the part of so many of us who urgently feel the need to translate into action our deeply felt concern for all that seems wrong in our human condition. Only through the wholehearted and unceasing offering of our hearts, our minds and our very souls to that point of Light which lies deep in the recesses of each one of us shall we find the illumination to *know beyond all doubt* the part we are to play in the fulfilment of the true destiny of our race—a destiny which shall be a newness and a glory beyond the power of present language to describe.

Chapter Four

"What can an imperfect man going in the midst of imperfect men achieve?"

—Sri Aurobindo

We live at a time of seeming confrontation in a marked degree between the forces of disintegration on the one hand, at many levels of our existence, and those of reintegration on the other. It would therefore in my view be difficult to overrate the supreme importance of our learning to share our insights and sense of involvement in regard to the crucial issue of the movement towards a unified humanity.

A striking fact of our present moment is that throughout the world a reappraisal is taking place about the origin and nature of the universe, and we seem to be in the very midst of a scientific revolution which, as it gathers momentum, may come to dwarf that which marked the revolutionary discoveries of Copernicus, which upset all common sense knowledge and the skilled observations of the leading astronomers and mathematicians of the time. Now and again we get stirring intimations of impending events of a dramatic kind, which may serve to jolt us for a time out of more conventional patterns of thought. We might take as an example a book written jointly by a Russian astronomer of the Soviet Academy of Sciences in Moscow and an American space scientist of Harvard University. The joint authors have never met and their collaboration—incidentally a pleasing individual witness to International Co-operation Year—has taken place by means of correspondence exchanged across the ideological frontiers. Their study is called "Intelligent Life in the Universe." It deals with the evolution of stars and planets and the beginnings of life on earth and reaches the conclusion that the earth has been visited by various galactic civilizations thousands of times in the course of its evolution and that an attempt is probably being made to contact us at this very moment.

These matters are relevant because it would clearly be vain to study approaches to human unity, and the creation of a planetary society, in a narrow perspective divorced from the total stream of our evolutionary development and from significant universal and cosmic facts which are widely impinging themselves upon our consciousness at this time. Although there may be need to give careful consideration to whatever institutions, frameworks and laws we may envisage for our world society, it is equally indispensable and even more important to direct our concern to the *spirit* of our world community in its individual and collective expression and in particular to the ways and means of effecting the release of those infinite divine resources which, like the power locked up in the atom, lie virtually asleep at the core of our individual being. It is an awakening of these latent powers which alone can give glory and meaning to life on earth. Without such an awakening any "peace" and "unity" brought about by external arrangements of a formal character will be without substance and will certainly not meet the deepest aspirations of the heart and soul of man.

I would like initially to examine briefly some of the thought and work which is to be encountered both in the East and in the West envisaging the emergence of an ideal society and heralding a new type of man and a new universal civilization.

Among the more significant movements of progressive thought and activity directed to the theme of a quality of human unity which would provide for the maximum spiritual growth is that which is to be found radiating outwards from the Sri Aurobindo Ashram at Pondicherry, India. This Ashram is now presided over by the Mother, who is also president of the movement World Union. World Union looks to "a mighty mobilization of hitherto scattered individuals and societies which are open to spiritual realities." It is especially concerned with the promotion of the ideas and ideals of Sri Aurobindo for the achievement of human unity. World Union speaks of "an awakening which marks the end of the dominance of materialism, ushers in the Spiritual Age and turns mankind from threatening disaster to its true destiny." The Mother, in direct and simple language, tells World Union that its task is to say to people everywhere: "The world is one. This is a fact. Let us become conscious of it and live up to this unity. It is not that unity needs to be brought in from outside and imposed upon it: it is just that the world is not conscious of its unity. It has to be made conscious. World Union's work is to spread the awakening by every means and by educating its members. It is the leaven to help raise society to meet the descending Light and Force. A new Force is now manifesting in the world which makes it possible for the world now to become conscious of its unity." Of Sri Aurobindo the Mother says: "You must remember that what Sri Aurobindo represents in world history is not a teaching, nor even a revelation. It is a decisive Action direct from the Supreme." To the 600 children being educated at the Ashram she says: "Do not aim for success. Our aim is perfection. Remember you are on the threshold of a new world, participating in its birth and instrumental in its creation. There is nothing more important than the transformation. There is no interest more worthwhile."

What, we may ask, is the meaning of this reference to "a new Force" and "a descending Light?" We recall to mind the Great Invocation or Prayer which has spread throughout the world and which is said to belong to no person or group but to all humanity. Translated into over 52 languages, it asks for the descent of Light, Love and Power to restore the Plan on earth, and for the wills of men to be guided by the Will and Purpose of God.

In one of Sri Aurobindo's major works, "The Ideal of Human Unity" (published by the Sri Aurobindo Ashram at Pondicherry), the author stresses throughout the ultimate inevitability of a spiritual order on earth. He writes: "A spiritualized society can alone bring about a reign of individual harmony and communal happiness: or, in words which though liable to abuse by the reason and the passions are still the most expressive we can find, a new kind of theocracy, the Kingdom of God upon earth, a theocracy which shall be the government of mankind by the Divine in the hearts and minds of men." In another passage he observes: "God works all his miracles by an evolution of secret possibilities which have been long prepared, at least in their elements, and in the end by a rapid bringing of all to a head, a throwing together of the elements so that in their fusion they produce a new form and name of things and reveal a new spirit. Often the decisive turn is preceded by an apparent emphasizing and raising to their extreme of things which seem the very denial, the most uncompromising opposite, of the new principle and the new creation." Sri Aurobindo envisages the ideal society as a field of relations which afford to the individual his opportunity for growing towards an ever greater state of perfection and sees the principle of social compulsion as a law of man's imperfection. Imperfect in itself, it must always be imperfect in its operation. Evolution must pass beyond man as it has passed beyond the animal. He envisages a decisive turn of mankind to the spiritual ideal. "This beginning," he writes, "may mean the descent of an influence that will alter at once the whole life of mankind in its orientation and enlarge for ever, as did the development of his reason and more than any development of the reason, its potentialities and all its structure."

Sri Aurobindo's view of man as a transitional being has great significance for our present moment and, while viewing this transformation into a new and higher species as an inevitable evolutionary development, he maintains that a change of this kind must necessarily first take place in the individual and in a great number of individuals before it can lay any effective hold upon the community. He stresses the importance of having faith in this spiritual conversion—to realize it every moment as a possibility. "The individuals," he observes, "who will most help the future of humanity in the New Age will be those who will recognize a spiritual evolution as the destiny and therefore the great need of the human being. Even as the animal man has been largely converted into a mentalized and, at the top, a highly mentalized humanity, so too now in the future an evolution or conversion of the present type of humanity into a spiritualized humanity is the need of the race and the intention of nature." Sri Aurobindo goes on to warn against the mistake of thinking that this change can be effected by outward institutions. A healthy unity of mankind can never, he says, be brought about by state machinery, whether it be by a grouping of powerful and organized states enjoying carefully regulated and legalized relations with each other or by the substitution of a single world state. There has to come about a transformation in the individual if it is to be made a reality for the race. It is not man's ascent into some remote heaven that is desired, but rather the ascent here and now into the Spirit and the descent of the Spirit into his normal humanity—the conversion of his whole life to the lead of the Spirit. The perfect society will be that which most completely favours the perfection of the individual, and the perfection of the individual will be incomplete if it does not help towards the perfect state of the society to which he belongs and eventually to that of the largest possible human aggregate, the whole of a united humanity.

Finally, Sri Aurobindo in "The Ideal of Human Unity" presents us with the alternatives of a world state founded upon the principle of centralization and uniformity—a mechanical and formal unity—and a world founded upon the principle of liberty and variation in a free and intelligent unity. One of the questions which I think we have to ask ourselves is whether we are to be concerned to expand our energies in building the former or to a rather greater extent to further the realization that there is a divine Reality, in which we are all one; that humanity is its present highest expression on earth; and that the human race and human beings are the means by which it will progressively reveal itself here in the world around us. Some of us may conclude that the higher hope of humanity lies in a growing number of people developing this realization in themselves, so that when we come to the point of finding mechanical solutions temporary and disappointing, the truth of the Spirit may reveal itself and lead humanity along the path of its highest possible happiness and perfection.

Here I would like to interject some reference to the subject of prophecy, which has moved like an unbroken thread through human history since the beginning of time and which is most evident in our day. Some may give it scant attention and yet it would be foolish and, I think, irrational to overlook the *fact* of the great number of intimations coming to us in the form of suggestions, beliefs and messages from all parts of the world and which point to the imminence of some great change in the human condition. These are interlinked with reports of supernormal—that is, hitherto not normally known—appearances and visions proclaiming in one form or another this coming change. About 35 years ago Sri Aurobindo, who was a giant in intellect and spirituality, declared that we were now moving ever nearer to a point of supreme radical change in the nature of man. Speaking of what he termed a new force, to which he gave the name "Supramental," he claimed that this force was already exerting itself on man's consciousness, "and would enter a phase of realizing power by 1967." There are other Eastern saints and sages who have marked this year as one having exceptional significance for the human race, and since 1961 the Universal Link, operating from a centre at St. Annes-on-Sea, Lancashire, England, has been independently circulating information on a worldwide scale indicating the existence, through revelation, of a "New Direct Link" now uniting mankind with his divine source, and of a great universal revelation of Light and Power which is to occur before the end of 1967. As an example of the force with which this idea of some great transformation is presenting itself I would like to share with you the following graphic description given by the Mother of the Sri Aurobindo Ashram of an inner experience relating to the breakthrough of the coming Light. She saw herself "as a form of living gold, bigger than the universe, facing a massive golden door which separated the world from the Divine. As I looked at the door, I knew and willed, in a single movement of consciousness, that the 'time has come,' and lifting with both hands a mighty golden hammer I struck one blow, one single blow on the door and the door was shattered to pieces. Then the Supramental Light and Force and Consciousness rushed down upon the earth in an uninterrupted flow."

I make no apology for having dwelt a little on the subject of revelation, which has always been the way man becomes conscious of that which with his own unaided reason he cannot discover for himself. I truly believe revelation has deep meaning for our time and any consideration of our theme would be incomplete were we to cast it aside as irrelevant. Our intuitive scientists call the same type of experience "illumination," and we know that some of the greatest scientific truths and discoveries have come to us in such a way. The Mother herself beautifully weaves together the scientific and religious approach to life in her single, brief exhortation to us to see our lives "as a purposive evolution and as a divinely ordained mission."

Among the majority of people there seems to be the firmly held belief that man unassisted is the "doer," the author of his actions, while in fact it is either guiding or compulsive forces which activate him in his thinking and doing. When this realization dawns, the life and activities of an individual become basically transformed and his supreme concern will be to find ways of linking more consistently with those higher forces which are directing his own evolution and that of the race of man as a whole.

Those who have made some acquaintance with the life and work of that eminent scientist and man of God, Pierre Teilhard de Chardin—undoubtedly one of the greatest contemporary thinkers—will realize how close is so much of his thinking to that of Sri Aurobindo. When we speak of a movement towards human unity we are again reminded, in the writings of Pierre Teilhard, that it is the evolutionary process to which we must turn our attention. All is contained in that. It is not safe to stop with humanity. We need always to look to that which is making humanity more than it now is. He affirms the present as marking a time of fulfilment of an evolutionary process begun some thousand million years ago. The course of man's evolution is basically directed towards a united and integrated humanity. Running through all his writings is the theme of genesis or becoming. A natural impulse is driving humanity towards what Pierre Teilhard calls "planetization." For Pierre Teilhard the Incarnation represents the means by which God's evolutionary purpose is being and will be achieved in spite of man's natural tendency to reject the call to union with God and his Creation. Pierre Teilhard calls the evolutionary process in its present phase the early stage of "Christogenesis"—the process by which all mankind is called to form the mystical Body of Christ. Man not only has a future in time but his development involves an inevitable movement towards ever higher states of spirituality and life expression. This is an evolutionary imperative if viewed as a process taking place in terms of the whole rather than of the individual element or group. Growth occurs through mutations or transformation points. Pierre Teilhard stresses the importance of grasping this perspective on evolution, which seen from close range appears continuous, while if one stands back a little all is discontinuous. One of Pierre Teilhard's conclusions which seems to me to have special relevance for us is that each stage of emergence is *an unprecedented newness* in relation to the stage before.

Pierre Teilhard shares with Sri Aurobindo and Professor Sir Julian Huxley, all among the greatest masters of contemporary thought, a similar view of a universal evolution moving towards a unique breakthrough of unimaginable breadth and depth. Expressing himself in different language, Professor Huxley envisages the evolutionary emergence of a wholly new species, a type of being as different from our present humanity as contemporary humanity differs from the highest type of animal life.

It may be difficult to judge the extent to which these insights we have been discussing are filtering through into the various educational media of different countries. We may find ourselves living and planning and educating our population in a largely uninformed and meaningless manner unless we take note of these implications. However, some comfort may be drawn from Pierre Teilhard's stirring remark, that "a truth once seen, even by a single mind, always ends up by imposing itself on the totality of human consciousness."

An educational revolution begins with educationists. Many of you will know of the New Education Fellowship (now renamed the World Education Fellowship) as an acknowledged growing point for enlightened teaching over the past 45 years. Their annual conference, attended by educationists from many countries, was this year* held at Chichester. The distinguished biologist, Professor Sir Alister Hardy, in his remarkable opening address entitled "New Perspectives on Human Destiny," made a powerful appeal for the building of what he called a scientific theology for the era which lies ahead of us, and on three separate occasions in the course of his address he reminded his audience of the dangers of dogmas of materialism which were supposedly based on secure scientific foundations. He remarked upon the fact that our civilization had been built upon a spiritual interpretation of the world, and that if the majority of people come to have a materialistic outlook the result could not be good. His concluding words stressed the need for "an experimental faith which can regenerate the spiritual power that has been the driving force of all the great civilizations in the past."

Professor Hardy, referring to Professor Sir Julian Huxley as his old friend and tutor when he was an undergraduate at Oxford, expressed concern that the idea of monism, which had grown up with the development of science, now threatened to dominate the world. He referred to a passage written by Professor Huxley in the preface to his book "Religion without Revelation," which reads: "This question of God or no God, external Power or no external Power, non-human values as against human evolving values—this question is fundamental"—and fundamental it would certainly seem to be. In an exchange of views between the two, Professor Huxley stated categorically that he was not a *materialist.* He was a *monist* in his belief that "we and the rest of life are products of, and agents in, a single process, the products having two aspects, material when observed from outside and subjective when viewed from inside." In "The Humanist Frame" Professor Huxley makes the observation: "Religion today is imprisoned in a theistic frame of ideas, compelled to operate in the realities of a dualistic world"; and in the Ninth Fawley Foundation Lecture, delivered in the University of Southampton in 1962, he states his own position in the following explicit terms: "The knowledge explosion of the last hundred years since Darwin is giving us a new vision of our human destiny—of the world of man, and of man's place and role in the world. It is an evolutionary and monistic vision, showing all reality as a self-transforming process...as a unitary and continuous process, with no dualistic split between soul and body, between matter and mind, between life and not-life, no cleavage between natural and supernatural: it reveals that all phenomena, from worms to women, fram radiation to religion, are natural."

As a scientific humanist Professor Huxley says that the need of our time is "a new, an integrated and compelling vision of human destiny." Now is there really, I wonder, an unbridgeable chasm between the theists on the one hand and the scientific humanists on the other? Personally I am convinced this will disappear with the raising of human consciousness to higher levels. From now onwards this process will be an increasingly rapid one and we shall see the emergence of the divine man.

At this point I believe the difference will largely be one of semantics. The new species, the new humanity which is now coming to birth, is indeed God-Man. For those with eyes to see, specimens of the New Man (God-Man) have long been among us as way-showers of our destiny. In this dawning age of enlightenment the Christian world will, I think, find itself ready to abandon the dualistic outlook. Content to view God as All in All—as the entire and infinite Evolutionary Process—this will be seen as gain rather than loss. Furthermore, as Truth and Divinity break through on a universal scale, as Transcendent and Immanent are brought together in this tremendous breakthrough, we shall see the end of religion as we have known it. It will have served its purpose. We are building the City of God on earth, the City of Resurrected Man. In the words of Sri Aurobindo: "At the end the flickerings of faith will cease, for we shall see His face and feel always the Divine Presence."

We know that the new order cannot be simply a framework of arrangements between national structures. If we are to help to further the aims and ideals of the United Nations Organization with the world-embracing unifying activities being achieved through the various agencies of UNESCO, shall we not need to gain practical recognition for the fact that it is *individual human beings* who comprise the stuff of which nations are made and who will in the last resort be required to make meaningful any world society which is brought to birth? *It is our own individual transformation* which needs particular attention, and it is our inherent capacity to be sensitive and receptive to the wisdom of the higher ranges of our being which needs encouragement and training. We know from the experience both of scientists and mystics that a breakthrough of truth is always at hand when the need is there and when we approach the problems before us in a quiet mood of sincere aspiration and attentiveness to the illumination that can come to us in a flash beyond the levels of the rational mind. Our acute problems resulting from conflicting ideologies, conflicting nationalisms, severe economic disparities and explosive racial tensions, the ever-present signs of man's inhumanity to man—these problems can only be solved from the perspective of a new consciousness and a universal and total view of man.

The transformation of our at present fragmented human society, with national sovereignty being especially disruptive of the true unity of the human family, is a supreme consideration calling for urgent discussion by individuals *in small concerned groups* and in the higher school grades and universities throughout the world. Such meetings are likely to be more fruitful when there is a sincere desire by those taking part to seek attunement with their own deep spiritual centre at the outset of the meeting. There is need for a wider appreciation of the importance of universal education in world citizenship. Although this subject is already being given some attention and the Council for Education in World Citizenship is doing remarkably fine work, the approach is still somewhat narrow and national attitudes tend to predominate in relation to the fundamentally human and universal consciousness and outlook which it is evidently so desirable to encourage.

To the universalist, language is essentially a means first and foremost of communication, and we cannot fail to favour every reasonable way of spreading understanding throughout the world as rapidly as possible. There would therefore seem to be a place for a neutral, non-national international language medium such as Esperanto. In 1954 the General Conference of UNESCO passed a resolution recognizing that the results attained by Esperanto are in accordance with UNESCO's aims and ideals and UNESCO has more recently increased its support for the promotion of this language. The teaching of Esperanto as an auxiliary language in all schools would greatly contribute to the linguistic unity of mankind. The annual congresses I have attended reflect wonderfully the spirit of human unity across national, racial and ideological frontiers.

I have mentioned the need for concerned people to meet in small groups. In fact, one of the encouraging signs of our time is the extent to which this is taking place. Many of these tiny groups, which are beginning to proliferate all over the world, started with a sense of isolation: but a linking up process is now taking place so that they are becoming increasingly aware of the existence of one another and of the power that could be manifested through them. A great number of them are spiritually orientated and seem consciously or unconsciously to be open to Sri Aurobindo's advice contained in the couplet:

"To change humanity first your erring shape of soul recast
Anon your eyes shall find nothing around remains unchanged at last."

Some of the world's foremost scientific and spiritual thinkers maintain that we are on the threshold of an evolutionary transformation which is almost if not absolutely unimaginable to our present state of consciousness and understanding. We are to find that God and Man are essentially one. Divinity is Man become truly conscious. A new type of humanity is now emerging, Universal Man, Divine Man. Man is in process of becoming a true spiritual being. Since no line of demarcation can scientifically be drawn between matter and that which is non-material, we may awaken to the realization that we have all along been in the throes of a spiritual rather than a material revolution from which is to flower a world society and a universal civilization. We might at least in some degree draw a comparison with the birth of a child as it emerges by means of a process which is not without shock and pain into an entirely new condition; or we might take the case of the emerging chick which, not without seeming effort and yet with the certainty of the evolutionary imperative, breaks through its shell into its wholly new environment.

There is no doubt that *humanity* will triumph. For ourselves as individual human beings the question is whether and in what degree we find ourselves receptive to the cosmic flow of power—the cosmic evolution—that is upon us, and whether and to what extent we concern ourselves with preparation for the transformation. Nothing else matters.

Chapter Five

I want to tell you a story which you may find as stirring and as enthralling as any to be encountered in the scriptures of any religion or in the lives of the mystics, past or present. These happenings which we are to consider are totally relevant for our time. They invite a response from all people everywhere. Indeed, different versions of the events related to the Universal Link Revelation exist in different countries because it is infinite in its ramifications and universal in its scope. There are, however, certain essential facts connected with it which I shall now endeavour to relate. May I first, however, make it clear that where opinions are expressed these do not necessarily reflect the views of anyone except myself or the person or persons specifically held to have expressed them. It is essentially for each of us individually to make up our own minds and come to our own individual insights about this matter. I do not think that any corporate body would even at this stage find it easy to venture a judgement in regard to what these reported experiences and events portend.

In September, 1964 Lt. Colonel T.R. Henderson, Ph.D., an independent investigator, delivered a scholarly address before the Churches' Fellowship for Psychical and Spiritual Studies at Somerville College, Oxford. His address, which he called "What is the Universal Link?" and from which he has kindly given me permission to quote, concluded as follows:

> "Here we seemingly have evidence of a movement of the Spirit on the waters of human consciousness. It may well be an expression of the moving of the Holy Spirit in human affairs in our time; possibly even a step in the evolution of a higher human consciousness on the way towards unknown goals. If our Fellowship has a divine mission in preparing people for that enlightenment that will bring them to the realization that 'the Kingdom of God is within us,' then surely a deeper study of the Universal Link is part of this mission, for it is possible that it may be the Direct Link of Self Realization at a very high level."

Although I am a life member of the Churches' Fellowship, and also a member of the Society for Psychical Research for over 30 years, it cannot be claimed that what follows consists of a "deeper study" so much as some additional material for meditation, prayer and personal decision. The very nature of the Universal Link Revelation does not in fact easily lend itself to the type of deep study which can readily be applied to less extraordinary psychical happenings and it did not wholly surprise me to learn that a team of investigators, appointed by the Society for Psychical Research, were unable to find anything which they considered to be sufficiently substantial for them to investigate. In this connection I shall, in what follows, unashamedly regard you as having powers of intuitive perception as real and valid as your powers of reason, and, after outlining the salient facts affecting these developments, I shall do my best to bring Colonel Henderson's 1964 statement up to date. Although I do not personally find myself in wholehearted agreement with *all* of his conclusions, his report is unquestionably of quite outstanding value in relation to what I consider to be by far the most significant spiritual and psychical events of our time.

On the 11th April, 1961, at a house called Bethany in Christchurch Road, Worthing, Richard Grave, a north of England businessman, who was at the time a self-acknowledged unbeliever in spiritual reality, had what I would describe as a Pauline experience. Richard, as I will now call him, had recently taken a lease on this house and was in the act of discarding an old picture on a religious theme, which he at the time regarded as rubbish left by his predecessor. While he was carrying the picture under his right arm towards the dustbin to throw it away, he was suddenly aware of a bearded Christ-like figure standing in front of him and blocking his path. The figure spoke and said: "I am He!" Then, reaching forth with his left hand, he touched the glass of the picture. In the explosion which followed, the glass was pulverized and driven in the tiniest fragments into the face of the picture. Simultaneously the figure disappeared in a brilliant blaze of orange light so powerful that in raising his left arm to shield his eyes from the intense glare Richard's forearm received a sharp burn. The picture, which from its darkened and blistered condition became within minutes of this incident perfectly restored, is entitled "The First Christmas Morn." It seems to bear no signature and is a representation of the Angels announcing the birth of Jesus Christ to the shepherds.

The picture was soon to become known as "The Weeping Angel of Worthing" and it attracted much attention in the ensuing months. Quite often drops of moisture would form, sometimes on the face of the Angel, at other times on other parts of the picture, and there seemed to be no natural explanation for this phenomenon. The water under analysis was found to be salt and of the consistency of human tears. The "weeping" on occasions was too copious to be due to condensation. There are letters on file from many individuals testifying to their experience of seeing the picture "weep" and on the 28th April, 1961, some drops appeared on the face of the foremost Angel while the cameras were being assembled for a live broadcast on Independent Southern Television. In the course of the broadcast the picture was shown, and the representative of Southern Television made it quite clear to viewers that drops of moisture from the face of the Angel had been witnessed by himself and others during the afternoon and just prior to the broadcast.

I should like at this point to introduce the name of Mrs. Liebie Pugh, who passed into what some of us would call the Greater Life on the 5th December, 1966, at the age of 78. She is known by a great number of people throughout the world simply as Liebie and it is as Liebie that I shall refer to her from now on. Many regard her as the architect, if not actually the founder of the Universal Link and so exceedingly complex is her involvement in the whole of these happenings that I must ask you to bear with me with great patience in any obscurities which may seem to arise as I proceed with this story. It would be all too easy to say too little about her, or too much. I think I may claim to have come into a close relationship with her during her last four years.

Colonel Henderson, who is himself a man of the widest spiritual understanding and experience, described Liebie in the course of his September, 1964, address as having undoubtedly for many years lived a life akin to Self Realization absorbed in the presence of God, and anyone who knew her at all well could scarcely fail to view her as a singleminded devotee of the spiritual life. She was found to be equally at ease in discussions on Religion, Theosophy, Christian Science, Spiritualism, various forms of Yoga, Subud, etc., and while a Roman Catholic she became the author of a booklet called "Abide in Me," which has been reprinted by the Catholic Truth Society and which is described on page 1 as having "for its sole object a deepened realization of union with our Divine Lord in any who are drawn to read it." Its keynote is summarized in the concluding paragraph of this little meditational booklet as follows:

"Let us get into the habit of hearing these words addressed as they are by Jesus Christ to each of us personally. *Let us hear them, see them, become saturated with them.* Let this incredibly gracious command dominate our whole life. These are his words to us:

ABIDE IN ME."

May we now revert to the events which were happening in Worthing in the month of April, 1961? Liebie at this time was living in a house situated only half a mile away from the scene of Richard's devastating and life-changing experience, and she came across a news item about it which appeared in the Psychic News of the 4th May. Until that time Liebie and Richard were quite unaware of one another's existence. Liebie at once made an appointment to call upon Richard and shortly afterwards he returned her call. It was in Liebie's house that Richard experienced a further shock. His eyes alighted upon a photograph of a plasticine model of a Christ-like being sculptured by Liebie three years previously and given the name "Limitless Love." It seems that the effect upon him when he saw it was electrifying and he exclaimed in great excitement: "This is the Master!" He appeared quite overcome. In reply to

Liebie's observation: "You mean it's something like Him?" Richard at once replied: "What do you mean 'something like?' It is Him. It's the Master as He comes."

After further exchanges in the course of which Richard emphasized the exact similarity of the representation, even to the hair style and the robes, Liebie concluded the conversation with the following revealing words (according to her notes taken at the time and incorporated in a documentary of these earlier events which she forthwith compiled):

> "Well I must accept what you say, Richard. It's difficult... I model a portrait of a head of all that I admired most, and you tell me three years later that this model of mine is a portrait of the Master who comes to you!"

At this point I should add in clarification that Liebie had been contacted some years previously by a noted sensitive, Katherine Hayward, who on higher direction requested her to model "a new head of the Master." This was the plasticine model to which I have just referred and which was duly completed by Liebie in 1958.

Let us now turn from "The First Christmas Morn" which seems to have been used as a kind of focal link for the initial appearances of this entity and seek some understanding of these continuing manifestations and what they may portend. In my world travels during the past few years I have been carrying with me a photograph of "Limitless Love." There seems to be considerable circumstantial evidence, in the widespread outpouring of spiritual forces which is now so marked, that people in whose sanity on acquaintance we would not be disposed to doubt, report having quite dramatic spiritual experiences. Many have reported to me seeing, and even having conversations with, an entity of similar appearance whom they claim to be perceiving, although probably in a raised state of consciousness, in solid form. However, we are now considering the particular case of Richard Grave, and the point of these preliminary observations is to indicate that though every experience of this kind is in a sense unique, Richard's experiences may well in some way or other denote what is happening, or what is liable to happen, universally. Indeed Liebie, one of whose functions was to be a worldwide reporter of these events to those who expressed a desire to be kept in touch with them, never tired of reiterating that the Universal Link was in no sense a *teaching*: it was *a universal operation.* The earlier events connected with this operation are reported in the documentary to which I have referred and in a series of further publications and news letters issuing first from Worthing and, after the autumn of 1961, from 1, St. George's Square, St. Annes-on-Sea, Lancashire. It was to this address that Liebie moved upon receiving a specific directive from the One appearing to Richard. This entity, soon after his initial appearances, became known as Truth, Limitless Love, the All-Knowing-One, interchangeably.

I think you may find it helpful as this story develops to bear in mind that when Richard, during the earlier appearances, asked the entity for its name, it replied: "Liebie knows My name." Sometimes the entity has been addressed as "Master" and according to Liebie this should be understood in the most realistic sense as applying to one who shows complete mastery—a mastery not known to normal man, but known to, and shown by, all the Masters who have visited mankind through the ages.

The messages to Richard, which often come in the form of directives, seem charged with a self-evident authority, which neither Richard nor Liebie have ever been disposed to question. Truth (as I shall henceforward call the entity) dictates his messages to Richard, who writes them down and invariably reads them over to his Cosmic Visitor while he is still present, to ensure their accuracy. During Liebie's earth life, an indispensable requirement of the operation was that Richard, as soon as possible after receiving a message, should at once report it to Liebie. Richard lives about two miles outside St. Annes in the direction of Blackpool and so this was normally no great burden.

Even from the earliest developments it seemed clear that these happenings, irrespective of any other factors in the situation, indicated a concern to draw attention to spiritual values in a world in which, to its seeming jeopardy, materialistic values are manifestly predominant.

Miss A.E. White, the Secretary of the Churches' Fellowship, in a most perceptive and sympathetic report which with her permission was included in the documentary compiled by Liebie of these early happenings, observed that their importance lay in the fact that they appeared to be something quite unique and at variance from other forms of psychic manifestation. They were in fact very difficult to fit into *any* of the recognized categories. They seemed neither to involve what is known as clairvoyance, on the part of Richard Grave, nor a materialization, since the entity was not visible to others who might be present. In this connection one of the messages is most revealing. It is this: "I do not build and rebuild My physical form when I appear to My medium. I am always present in full form. My Whole Self is never divided." Such conceptions are difficult to our three dimensional minds, and illumination through prayer or meditation is perhaps our best hope of coming to some understanding of what is here being conveyed. Miss White remarked upon the apparent strangeness that someone so uninformed on the subject should have been chosen, though she pertinently points to the experience of St. Paul on the Damascus Road and poses the question whether the people of his day regarded him as the most suitable person to be chosen to take Christianity to the Gentiles.

Among the earlier messages of Truth is one which reads as follows:

"Reveal your experiences to the elders and leaders of the Church and from that moment I will urge them too."

Richard had already and most eagerly rung up the nearest clergyman as one might ring up a doctor after an accident because, as he subsequently explained to me, he felt in those first moments that the wires had been crossed and that this was not a matter for him at all! So when he received this later directive he enthusiastically reduced his experience to writing in a frank and respectful letter addressed to the Archbishop of Canterbury. It would, however, be rather like looking for a needle in the proverbial haystack to find signs of any noticeable response on the part of the Churches during the past few years and it remains an open matter whether in fact no "urging" has taken place or whether there is some reluctance on the part of the Christian Churches to face and examine the revolutionary implications of these happenings.

Apart from the actual statements of Truth, which for many seem to have a compelling validity once it has been decided to examine them with an intuitive insight as well as through the window of reason and religious conviction, there seem to be at least six unusual events occurring almost simultaneously:

1. The appearance of the supernormal entity and his continuing and frequent appearances for a period of over six years.

2. The touch of the entity causing the glass to be pulverized while the picture was still held under the right arm.

3. The disappearance of the entity in a blaze of orange light.

4. The left hand, upraised as a shield against the light, being burnt enough to require a dressing.

5. The almost instantaneous restoration of the picture.

6. The persistent intermittent "weeping" on the face of the Angel and from other parts of the picture, a manifestation which still occurs though now at ever rarer intervals.

One would imagine that the odds against this combination of events occurring together must be extremely high, and the fact that these happenings should still be continuing must surely deserve our serious attention.

Colonel Henderson, to whose address I am continually referring because no other report exists which is anything like so valuable and comprehensive, has remarked that the most impressive thing immediately apparent to any visitor to Liebie Pugh is the powerful focus of spiritual power built up within her room. A great many individuals from different countries have testified to this, bearing witness to spiritual experiences which have come to them in this room at St. Annes-on-Sea, often though not invariably in her presence. Many of these experiences are relatable to Liebie's plasticine relief model of a pair of hands holding a chalice, which came to be known as "The Font" and it is thus referred to in the following directive dictated to Richard on the 22nd June, 1962:

> "The time is now opportune for all of My units to form themselves into a physical organization whereby they may unite with each other broadly towards a better understanding of the final Universal stage. The organization will be known simply as the Universal Link and no one is excepted from membership... All must be invited to St. Annes to touch My Font and experience My Vibrations so that they may each become My harbinger."

A number of people have held the Font and have experienced nothing exceptional. Colonel Henderson, however, is one of many who had remarkable experiences in the course of his investigation at St. Annes, which are worth alluding to because he did not include them in his address to the Churches' Fellowship which, for the most understandable reasons, he wanted to present in the most objective way possible. I now have his generous permission to give an account of them which is taken from a report received by him at the time and included in one of Liebie's news letters. Incidentally, I hope none of us is unduly reserved about the idea of the mystical. The Oxford Dictionary defines a mystic as one who seeks by contemplation and self-surrender to obtain union with or absorption into the Deity, or who believes in spiritual apprehension of truths beyond the understanding. In this sense I would say, from all that seems to be taking place at this time, and from my own experiences, that we are entering the mystical age on a universal front whether we choose to acknowledge it or not. This contention would seem to find support from a remark made one day by Truth that "every unit on this earth plane is a medium."

In the last week of November, 1962, Colonel Henderson arrived in St. Annes-on-Sea to investigate these happenings and questioned Liebie and Richard in great detail. He subsequently reported finding them completely co-operàtive. Under a powerful magnifying glass he examined the surface of the picture, "The First Christmas Morn," and found fragments of glass in many places. While he was wondering whether the "weeping" could be caused by moisture condensing where minute fragments of the broken glass remained embedded in the surface of the picture it began, as if in answer to his silent question, to exude tiny drops of water in the top left hand corner (a) away from the Angel, and (b) where there were no glass fragments, thus indicating that the moisture did not collect on glass fragments and neither did it necessarily come from the face of the Angel. After all these years the phenomenon remains unexplained and until some more mundane explanation is forthcoming we are left with the explicit message of Truth: "I have created the divinity within the picture." Colonel Henderson later leaned over the picture, which he had placed on the table before him, and told Liebie that he found himself "inhaling happiness" from it. That was the only way he was able to describe this particular experience. He reported perceiving the happiness coming to him from the picture just as scent is inhaled from a flower.

On another occasion during his visit, and after a period of meditation, Colonel Henderson picked up the Font and held it in front of him. Later he told Liebie there appeared to be milk within it and that this reminded him of the words: "As newborn babies desire the sincere milk of the word that ye may grow thereby." He reported then seeing the tips of the fingers of the two hands draw together over the Font and touch and then open again, and then draw together and again open. When he told Liebie this, she asked him if his eyes were open and he said: "Yes." The following exchanges then took place:

> Liebie: "You actually *saw* the fingers close and open, close and open?"
> Col. Henderson: "Yes. It indicated to me an unfolding."
> Liebie: "Do you believe the plasticine moved?"
> Col. Henderson: "No. I would say I was attuned to a state where my third eye was perceiving a fact on the inner plane."

Although I was not personally present when any of these incidents took place, my first visit to St. Annes-on-Sea did in fact overlap that of Colonel Henderson and on that occasion I recall remarking to Liebie that I felt myself to have been travelling *in the spirit* of the Universal Link for at least three years, meeting and speaking with individuals and small groups and addressing myself for the most part to the theme of the human race as one family under God. I even remember asking Liebie point blank whether there was any copyright on the name "Universal Link," which so perfectly seemed to describe my own chosen work and activity! I was soon to learn how very much more than this the Universal Link Revelation implied and embraced!

In the last few years there have been intimations from a number of sensitives in different parts of the world about events soon to take place in the heavens, or in the skies. I want to mention at this point Kathleen Fleming, a much and widely loved sensitive. For some years she lived at 1, St. George's Square, in a flat above that which was occupied by Liebie. Kathleen has been the conscious instrument for many remarkable messages and has often reported seeing the same entity as Richard, also in solid form. On the 8th February, 1964, she received the following message:

> "The Herald in the Sky is none other than a superimposed picture relayed from space. We shall let down enough substance to give a complete picture. Every human being will be attached by his particular vibration and everyone will simultaneously receive a shock of power. In this way everyone will receive My

Substance. It is not any catastrophe. They will all receive a full charge of this power which is already operating in a degree on earth and on the Day there will be a moment when *the whole earth will stop because of the power.*

The Herald will appear not very high above the earth. Four or five miles. It will appear solid and will be photographed. There will be music from it and MY VOICE shall be heard speaking to My people. All shall hear but not everyone will understand.

It will split through space. This time it will not be 'the Word was made flesh'; it will be that flesh will hear the word—the sound of love, for it will have its full attributes, sound, colour, form, density, substance, life—the universal energy.''

Kathleen then reported seeing the Herald, as it were, like a canopy over the earth, spread out and of enormous dimensions.

It is sometimes remarked that reports of the Universal Link Revelation, with its immense implications if it be valid, can only be reaching a comparatively tiny minority of the world's people. This view fails to take into consideration the multiplicity of often quite small meditational and prayer groups, perhaps consisting of no more than three or four people regularly meeting together, which have been mushrooming up on a worldwide scale in a kind of spiritual explosion, almost as if in counteraction to the atomic counterpart. The power of the word is great and no doubt it needs to be, as it were, horizontally communicated: but the universal explosion or downpouring of the Spirit and of Grace at this time is unquestionably a fact. I think you will nevertheless be interested in a story I want to tell you about the physical means by which these happenings have been reaching beyond ideological barriers into the socialist states of Eastern Europe.

One day in April, 1963, Truth appeared to Richard and said: ''Be prepared for a journey to Prague where you will reside for five days.'' Richard had no contacts in Czechoslovakia but he made arrangements to leave on the day indicated and on the evening of the 10th May, 1963, he checked in at the hotel room reserved for his appointed five day visit to Prague. Of course he had no plans of any kind, but soon after arriving at his hotel, immigration officials called to see him in connection with his papers which did not seem to be in order. Eventually this matter was cleared up and for the remainder of his time in Prague Richard gratefully accepted the daily hospitality of the communist officials. He was driven to Lidice which, as many of you know, had been turned into a place of perpetual pilgrimage after its total desecration and destruction by the Nazi regime. Here he found himself standing in front of a memorial which completely electrified him, with its gigantic wooden cross which Richard estimated to be about 40 feet high, around which had been placed a huge circle of *barbed wire* on the orders of Marshal Zhukov.

The symbol of the Cross and Circle had become completely familiar to Richard since Truth's early visits, and he had actually been required by Truth to draw the symbol and later even to cut it out in paper. His immediate reaction on seeing this gigantic cross was to exclaim out loud and he involuntarily found himself telling the communist officials the entire story of his unique experience. His new friends thereupon asked Richard if he would be willing to record his experiences for them on a tape. This he duly did in the form of question and answer. His communist friends later insisted on driving Richard to the airport and seeing him off home laden with gifts for himself and his wife and his two little girls.

There is a most interesting sequel to this story. About ten days after returning from his visit Richard sought an opportunity to ask for enlightenment as to its meaning. The reply came: "My son, your visit to Prague was within My Plan. All is well. The level of activity at this moment is wide and universal. There are many levels of understanding involved, all of which are representative of the compound metaphysical metamorphosis. Throughout I Am." Those of us who are aware of Richard's utter simplicity of expression and of his own down to earth vocabulary may well, I think, be excused a thoughtful smile!

All I can do in the course of a comparatively brief account of a subject so vast and all embracing is to leave you with a flavour of what this is all about, which might help perhaps to sharpen a little your own individual capacities for response. Before I conclude I feel I must share with you an aspect of this remarkable matter which it would not be right to omit. Some of you may think that in what I am now about to tell you we are adding needless complications to a series of phenomena which already tend to tax our understanding to the limit. In all this, however, we need to bear in mind that our likes and dislikes and the desire to resist disturbances to previously held concepts need to be subordinated to our supreme concern for Truth. Truth in fact seems quite unconcerned with what *beliefs* people hold. There is on the part of this entity a concern simply to communicate the *fact* of what is happening and the *fact* that *all is well,* a phrase which is continually being interspersed throughout the messages. It is indicated that human views and beliefs neither bring about, nor hinder, these New Age manifestations.

There is sufficient circumstantial evidence linked with Richard's own testimony that in the early days of these appearances Richard's normal vision was completely and permanently changed so that Liebie's physical appearance *to him* became identical with the bearded figure portrayed in the photograph of Limitless Love. He came to see them as one and the same, except for the way the lower part of Liebie was clothed. During her earth life a great many messages and directives were delivered personally to Liebie which throw considerable light upon her earth function and it was neither desired nor desirable that attention should be drawn to the personality aspect in this connection.

It is considered desirable to mention this now only to the extent that we are seeking to the utmost of our capacities some understanding of what all this means. It became inevitable that some hitherto undisclosed messages should come into the open after the appearance of an unusual term in a message which Richard one day publicly read out in the presence of 33 people assembled at 11 a.m. in Liebie's sitting room at St. Annes-on-Sea. It was Sunday, 4th December, 1966, and the message had been dictated to Richard at 9.55 that morning, the day before Liebie was *officially* certified as having withdrawn from her physical body. I have to put it this way because of information contained in a later message to the effect that the true withdrawal took place around noon on the 4th December. The morning message runs as follows:

"This is the last propinquity meeting in the presence of *My earth entity.* Today you will talk freely among yourselves until 11.55 a.m. at which time you will observe five minutes silence and meditation. At the hour of 12 noon you will resume discussion. THIS IS A MIGHTY PHASE OF MY WHOLE OPERATION AND EXERCISE."

When Richard wrote this message down he was directed to write the last eleven words in capital letters, and this is perhaps the place to remark that he was always shown when to write in capitals: the word "MY" was invariably written in capitals as if God himself was speaking.

Many of those present on this occasion wondered, of course, what was meant by the term "My earth entity," while to others, who had already through their own experiences shared some of Richard's unique insights, this choice of words did not come as any great surprise or shock. You will now, I think, be ready to hear the following message which was dictated in the usual way to Richard with the intimation that it was addressed to Liebie:

"Henceforth I shall discuss you and I as one. The Father has now, of late, created you into a separate and direct earth unit for the express purpose of sole control of all earthbound factors. The Father has chosen us to communicate with the Universe and prepare the way for the Revelation. When the Father has completed the Universal Link you and I will become ONE. Our function will be that of the direct light and directive for the Universe. The two forms as seen by Our Medium (Richard) are but one. Our Whole Self is never divided. Your every reflection IS the Master. Only MY WHOLE SELF will be kept invisible until THE DAY. Until then, many will see aspects of Me in many forms, all of which are throughout the fullness of Me. The outward expression of My earth being is simply the using of all that energy that circulates from Me. It is vital to My Universal Progress that a continuity of link vibrations is maintained through MY ONE AND WHOLE BEING."

Towards the close of 1961, when the above message was delivered, Richard was told: "You will never see the old face again." It was then that his vision was permanently changed. At the same time the following message came for Liebie:

"My medium can now see the fullness of Me in My earth being which shall remain for all time."

It is evident that many more questions are being raised in our minds by these disclosures than any of us can profess to have easy answers for. It may be that we shall need to rest content with our own individual understanding of these happenings. One question which leaps at once to the mind is why, if Liebie was a being of such great spiritual magnitude and the "earth entity" of one so All Knowing, did she appear in her normal expression to be so completely cut off from this all knowing consciousness, needing to be continually kept abreast of things through the mediumistic capacity of Richard Grave? I do not propose to attempt a direct answer to this question and I certainly do not profess to know all the answers in relation to these extraordinary happenings. I did, however, once hear something which might perhaps throw some light upon this question. Katherine Hayward, the noted sensitive, to whom I have already referred, told me that when she first visited Liebie Pugh she heard herself, to her own astonishment, saying that the vibrational rate of Liebie's physical body was higher than that of anyone who had ever lived on earth. This if true would mean that the ratio between her consciousness and the vibrational rate of her body would need to be of an order that would permit her to discharge the specific function or functions for which she had become incarnate at this time, without experiencing an unduly expanded state of consciousness, which might interfere with the degree of physical contact that it was essential for her to maintain with the earth frequencies in order to enable her effectively to communicate and radiate the particular vibrational energies essential to her mission. This mission seemed to include the raising of the consciousness, by their response, of those who made contact with her.

Colonel Henderson, in the course of his 1964 address to the Churches' Fellowship for Psychical and Spiritual Studies, advanced the interesting and thought provoking hypothesis that the entity known as Truth or Limitless Love was, in fact, Liebie herself in the form of a "constellated fragmentation of her own personality," though because of the archetypal nature of the entity it was enabled to act as a symbol of very great power, calling up immense forces from the universal unconscious and even perhaps effecting a direct link with the Divine Ground itself. In this way fundamental truths might well come through in the heart of the messages though, in the view of Colonel Henderson, there would almost certainly be contamination of the truth due to what he calls psychological secretions.

It is true, of course, that normally a certain amount of colouring is to be expected in the processes by which messages, possibly of a high spiritual origin, are channelled through the consciousness of sensitives into the form of verbal messages or directives. One of the most illuminating ways in which I have heard this expressed is in the following phrase which came to a certain sensitive: "I reach you through *your* level of consciousness, not through *My* level of consciousness." In the case of Richard Grave, however, we need to reckon with the fact that, because of the unique mechanics of the operation, his own consciousness is virtually not a factor in the situation and interference by his own mental processes is reduced to an absolute minimum. On the whole question of the capacity of our consciousness to interpret and understand, a revealing little interchange took place between Truth and Richard on the 5th March, 1967. Richard asked: "Can we know a little more about the changes you have in mind and can we have some more information relative to the 'times'?"; to which Truth replied: "Not knowing is not—*is not*—a matter of being kept in the dark. Knowing is knowing when knowing is comprehensible."

With regard to the notion that the entity appearing to Richard may be a "constellated fragmentation" of Liebie's own personality, I do not profess to be an expert in these matters of psychological interpretation, but if this entity is held to be an extension or a projection—a secondary personality—of Liebie, it seems at least to be equally arguable (and my intuition does not contend against the supposition) that Liebie was an extension or a projection—a secondary personality if you like—of Truth or Limitless Love. We cannot in fact avoid the question: "What is Truth and where does Reality lie?" It surely depends precisely where in consciousness we hold our identity.

A learned friend of mine has pointed out to me that there is a great deal in the whole of this affair which is reminiscent of the stories relating to angels in the Old Testament. He refers me to the story of Abraham in Genesis, of Samson in Judges, to the Book of Tobit in the Apocrypha and also to the first chapter of the Epistle to the Hebrews in the New Testament. Angels act as emissaries of God and like prophets often speak in the first person singular in the name of the Lord. According to the Bible every individual and every nation has an angelic counterpart and in the Book of Revelation it is interesting to note that the communicator describes himself as the Angel of Jesus. The marks of an angel, according to ancient descriptions, include the following: appearance in all respects like a human being and just as solid; association with light, fire or flame; capacity for speech on ordinary mundane matters and for giving advice and instructions; ability to perform apparent wonders; unwillingness to give a name or to be known by a name.

The Universal Link Revelation is, as I have said, a matter about which we shall have individually to make up our minds. In conclusion I would therefore like to share with you the insights I found myself expressing during the propinquity meeting held at St. Annes-on-Sea on the 4th December, 1966. My remarks were triggered off by the expression "My earth entity" used in the message received that same morning by Richard. The view I then expressed is that Limitless Love and Truth have appeared and are still appearing in many forms in different parts of the world and the particular form appearing to Richard is one with Liebie, as Liebie is one with that form. An operation is taking place in the universe and the particulars about this universal operation are what the Universal Link Revelation is all about. Many people realize that we are on the threshold of a New Age—a New Dispensation—and the world will evidently not long continue in the way in which day to day living everywhere is now going on. Various speakers and writers have expressed this realization in different terms. Pierre Teilhard de Chardin, the eminent man of God and scientist, speaks of the divinisation of the world and the Christification of man as the phase we are now collectively beginning to experience. It is scarcely surprising that all religious, political, social and economic forms are breaking down to make way for the building of the Kingdom of God on earth. It is open to us to give ourselves to this Christing process as *conscious instruments* for the rule of Limitless Love and Truth. Who can tell what precisely is going to happen in the time ahead? It is, however, a fact that Limitless Love is appearing with ever greater frequency in the actions and to the vision of more and more people.

There may be many ways of intimating Liebie's function. Whatever else she may have been doing she was undoubtedly grounding tremendous energies which produce transformation and change. In the recorded experiences of a great number of people there emerges overwhelming evidence that what appeared as Liebie and what appeared in the picture of Limitless Love are one and the same and Liebie's withdrawal from her physical body, a planned part of the total operation, has of course in no way affected the appearances to Richard which still continue. Truth's emphasis in the Universal Link operation has been on the fact of his Power now proceeding through the Universe at an ever-increasing tempo in preparation for his Self-Revelation. Through the years we have had on the one hand the whole range of Truth's appearing, culminating in what he now calls his "advanced and final Showing," and on the other hand we have our human endeavours, through every form of aspiring thinking that appeals to us, *to respond.*

We are without question in the time of the winding up of human history as we have hitherto known it. We are in the very throes—the death throes of the old and the birth pangs of the new—of the "Second Coming." Says Truth: "I mean the New Age by the Coming Again." This may not take place in the way many of us have been led to expect, or perhaps I should say that we would be wise not to feel limited to any conventional image of its expression. This does not mean that the biblical prophecies are not to be fulfilled in one form or another. They are already being fulfilled and we are reaching the climax sooner than many of us expect. We need especially to learn from the lesson of Pentecost to expect the unexpected.

Let us be content to accept that in bringing his Divine Plan to fruition "God works in a mysterious way." We are now seeing a vast array of witnesses springing up and testifying to the factual nature of visions and revelations of all kinds, and for Christians to continue to think that the final Revelation of God has been given once and for all time may well serve as a block to a full understanding of everything that is now going on. In one message Truth speaks of "the Link necessary for the *completion* of My Coming to the Universe" and another says: "To effect My Materialization I require many instruments and this will create, to an extent, confusion." We can catch a glimpse of ways in which this confusion and division is possible when we reflect upon the seemingly inconsistent claims of the sincere devotees of the many illumined souls, incarnate and discarnate, whose supreme mission it is to fulfil the role referred to in the above message and also to bring their followers ultimately to an inward realization of the One Immanent and Transcendent God—Brahman—the One with countless names, who yet cannot be named—the ALL IN ALL. Christians know him through his only beloved Son, and since spiritually the whole is in the part—the Father is in the Son—and God gives himself totally to each of his children, it should not surprise those of us who know God in the Person of Jesus to learn that each of the gurus of India is truly God to their own devotees, and that what we generally know as Christianity is not the only acceptable way to the Godhead. The Mother of the Sri Aurobindo Ashram in Pondicherry, India, could write in her diary after meeting for the first time that great illumined saint and sage Sri Aurobindo: "It matters not if there are hundreds of beings plunged in the densest ignorance. He whom we saw yesterday is on earth: his presence is enough to prove that a day will come when darkness will be transformed into light, when Thy reign shall be indeed established upon earth." The Mother was regarded by Sri Aurobindo as sharing with him one and the same consciousness, and we have these further words which the Mother said came to her direct from God: "I have chosen thee from all eternity to be My exceptional representative upon the earth, not in an invisible and hidden way, but in a way apparent to the eyes of all men. And what thou wert created to be, thou shalt be!" The Mother could also say: "Since the beginning of the earth, wherever and whenever there was possibility of manifesting a ray of Consciousness, I was there." Sri Aurobindo and the Mother saw their work as involving "a decisive Action direct from the Supreme"—the manifestation of a new Force which will make it possible for the world to become conscious of its unity. This Force will also bring about the divinisation of the physical continuance in the material world through the descent of a supramental consciousness which Sri Aurobindo many years ago predicted would "enter a phase of realizing power" by 1967.

Other great ones, such as Meher Baba who, like Sri Aurobindo, was regarded by his followers as the last avatar, may be viewed, I suggest, as Cosmic Masters preparing those brought within their sphere of spiritual influence for the Day of Revelation, the Day of Manifestation, which will mark the Christing of the whole earth and the true beginning of the Golden Age—the Rule of Love and Truth. These and other spiritual lights are appearing in their astral and etheric counterparts in visions and dreams to those who are attuned to them. Prominent among these is the one who at birth was given the cosmic name Sun Myung Moon. Sun Myung Moon took earthly form in Korea in 1920, and after Jesus had appeared to him when he was 15 years old he accepted his own unique mission in relation to the "Second Coming" and he founded what he called the Unification Church of World Christianity. After spending a month in Korea as his guest, I can myself testify to the remarkable revelations which come to those who are attuned to him. It seems to me that because Sun Myung Moon is incarnate upon the earth at this time *and has a particular link with the Christ Ray,* he makes an indispensable bridge for many people who are being given exceptional and life changing experiences by taking his powerful name into their meditations.

How can we, then, best prepare ourselves for this climax of events which is so soon to occur? As I said at the beginning, the Universal Link Revelation is going forth by word and by the activity of the Holy Spirit to all who are open to receive it. It is, like the basic teaching of Jesus Christ, available not only to those who have come to call themselves Christians but to all men, women and children everywhere.

It does not seem to me to be adequate to dismiss this Revelation with the advice of Gamaliel as given in Chapter 5 of the Acts of the Apostles. It is surely not enough simply to say: "Let these people alone. If this movement is merely human it will collapse of its own accord, whereas if it is of God it cannot be overthrown." These events have been continuing and extending their scope for several years and I earnestly hope that more attention will be given to this matter in the time that remains, if only to ensure that as many people as possible are as prepared as possible to be as responsive as possible to what Truth has called "My Great Universal Revelation."

Let us be more concerned rather to *halt* than to *exercise* the activity of our *intellect* in regard to these things. Realization thinking—spontaneous knowledge—these are the keynotes to the New Age and to our transformed condition. Perhaps the best we can do individually is meditate and pray about the tremendous things we have considered together here, and earnestly seek an answer to the question: "ARE THESE THINGS TRUE?" We are assured that to all who persevere in sincere seeking an answer will be given. Those of us who are aspiring to live and follow the teaching and example of Jesus Christ should, it seems to me, above all else take care to guard against the holding of any concept or view about these things which might tend, however remotely, to place a limit on the Love, Power and Saving Grace of God for the whole of His Creation.

The following is a selection of the sayings dictated to Richard Grave by the One who has been appearing to him in solid form since 11th April, 1961.

During this period a great number of messages have been given of a personal and universal nature, and this All Knowing One is reported to be manifesting with messages of a confirmatory nature to an increasing number of individuals throughout the world.

1. I am the Truth, the Light, the All throughout the Universe.

2. Many will see aspects of Me in many forms, all of which are throughout the fullness of Me.

3. I have given unto the Universe many Manifestations of My Presence this century.

4. There will be many and more substantial manifestations to follow so that the prophecy of My Coming may remain kindled. There are many who are aware of My Presence among them. They can do nothing to enhance My Full Manifestation except hold faith and proceed in their own light until I am ready.

5. My Coming Again—this refers to the new vibration and divine energy that is feeding My Universe at this moment. I mean the New Age by the Coming Again. I have always been with the Universe in stage development which constituted My First Showing: now I am in My Last and Final Showing.

6. No one can know the day nor hour when My Great Universal Revelation will be enacted. However, by the first second of the first hour of Christmas morning, 1967, I will have revealed Myself to the Universe through the medium of nuclear evolution. This is My Plan which is absolute. There will be many who will receive their own confirmation and who will be moved to contact you. All is well. (9th September, 1962.)

7. Many people will be urged to make contact with St. Annes. These contacts will stretch across continents and include many levels of understanding. (27th January, 1963.)

8. Have no thought towards the seeming confusion of others around you. All is in My Universal Plan. Although the time is opportune for a physical Universal Link to be formed among those inspired, it must be remembered that all must walk only in the light that reflects Truth to them.

9. In the course of My whole Universal Operation My sole power flows through all of My earth units in varying degrees.

10. The lifting of the veil means the lifting of that veil which prevents complete universal sight, so allowing Me fully to be perceived by all My Universal units.

11. The orange flame that My instrument (Richard) sees is the All Power of Me which will now reflect from time to time.

12. (Richard asked: "Can you throw some light upon this question of others having seen you in a manner particular to them?") It is quite true others have seen and heard Me in and through their own perceptive powers. Everyone's power of perception depends upon whether they can clarify My direct vibration. To some it is difficult; to others like yourself it is easy by virtue of the receptive elements being stronger. This does not in any way mean that My power or vibration of My power is any less or greater throughout the whole operation either to you or to others. It simply means that to some I give a particular faculty amounting to contact.

13. I give what is required when it is required.

14. I do not build and rebuild My physical form when I appear to My medium. I am always present in full form.

15. My Whole Self is never divided.

16. I am most active on all planes and many things will become evident through the medium of others both on and off My Link. All subjects are on My Link by degree, some being on My level of Vibration.

17. It is vital to My Universal Progress that a continuity of Link vibrations is maintained through My One and Whole Being.

18. I create All and direct All. There is nothing beyond My reach whether personal or universal. I can halt or proceed any matter at all. Nothing is thrust upon Me.

19. The volume of power circulating at this moment from Me is great and coincides with human level scientific energies being spent. Recent nuclear tests and preparations are consistent with My warnings of some time back when I revealed the necessity for intervention in scientific matters. Such will be the case. My whole energy is released. I control all aspects of universal and personal function.

20. Pay no regard to those who question you and profess their

scepticism. They will know of your experience through the medium of other greater revelations and so they will seek you out in reconciliation.

21. Take heed of Me and know Me fully.

22. A full and detailed directive will be given about healing centres when I am ready.

23. My increased energy is circulating and may cause certain havoc which is within my arrangements.

24. I will intervene in many matters of science. A great many scientists are aware of an energy that is influencing their thesis.

25. To effect My Materialization I require many instruments and this will create, to an extent, confusion. Much deliberation is therefore necessary among My true followers so that they may tread wisely.

26. Reveal your experience to the elders and leaders of the Church. They will respond and from that moment I will urge them too.

27. If I were to return in peace no one would recognize Me except My re-incarnate. The multitude will have to recognize Me through a medium of might.

28. All are free to walk in that path which reflects Truth to them. My Plan is absolute. Nothing can halt it. All is well.

29. The time is nigh when all will know Me. Universal events on a human level will shortly leave nothing to the imagination. (15th January, 1967.)

30. There will be many outward signs in the course of the next few months which will awaken many. (30th January, 1967.)

31. Time is of little consequence now. As night approaches day may never come. Instead, the light will pour forth from the Father's House so that it will be likened to a more familiar glare and as if man had caused it.

32. My Whole Self will be kept invisible until **THE** DAY.

33. A major world conflict will herald the last stage of the Universal Progress. In the meantime general world conditions will show evidence of a leading up to the introduction of a nuclear device that will bring about the final human level episode. The major conflict I speak of will be between nations and it will be most sudden. A war will start in Asia and spread to the Western

World. A human press-button device will be used and, simultaneously with the pressing of the button, instead of disaster, the Universal Revelation will occur. (13th November, 1961.)

34. I have never used the word obedience in My directives. I have repeatedly stated that *all* must react according to their own clear inclinations and exercise the *free will* vested in themselves. *All* are free to walk in that path and light which reflects Truth to them in the full knowledge that they are loved and understood without any exception whatsoever. My directives are designed to direct— not to enforce or dictate a way of life whereby suffering and concern may be the outcome. (5th March, 1967.)

35. I am with you always.

The Coming Changes

Chapter Six

Letters and reports which have been reaching us recently reflect a serious and growing interest in both physical and telepathic contact with extra-terrestrial intelligence. In addition to the scientific project C.E.T.I. (Communication with Extra-Terrestrial Intelligence), a predominantly Czecho-slovak initiative, there has recently been world publicity about unidentified, crescent-shaped flying objects observed over Russia at a height of 30 miles, travelling at a speed of over ten thousand miles an hour. Reports of these sightings, mostly over the southern part of the Soviet Union (the Ukraine, the Crimea, the Caucasus), have been given publicity by Professor Felix Zigel of the Moscow Aviation Institute together with the statement that the UFO phenomenon constitutes a challenge to mankind and that it is the duty of scientists to accept this challenge. Revealing that a big team of scientists and specialists in the U.S.S.R. began a systematic study of the UFO question in 1967, Professor Zigel claims that the UFO "problem" has assumed universal dimensions and therefore calls for global research. It seems that many of the UFO forms observed in the U.S.S.R. fit into the classification of these objects accepted in the West. It is, however, unfortunate (as the Russian scientist points out) that certain scientists both in the Soviet Union and in the U.S.A. "deny the very existence of the problem instead of helping to solve it."

In view of the attention universally being drawn to this subject, we think it might be of interest to our readers to publish a remarkable message dictated in January, 1962, by the entity, apparently from another dimension, who appears in solid form to Richard Grave in England—known by the name of Truth, Limitless Love or the All Knowing One. This message is uniquely different in content from other messages from the same source and its implications are possibly more acceptable now—at least by the more open minded—than at the time the message was first delivered. It runs as follows:

"On Friday, February 7th, 1958, at 2.57 a.m. G.M.T. and at a point East of Moscow, a Russian scientist communicated with the pilot of a Martian scout craft by means of arm signals while the craft hovered only 18 feet above ground level.

On Saturday, April 11th, 1959, at 7.13 p.m. G.M.T. a team of Russian scientists established the first and only inter-planetary radio contact with the planet Mars. The Martians penetrated the polar region by means of sound waves carried by meteorites that are characteristic in the polar region of Russia. These sound waves

69

have now been successfully intercepted by the Soviet inter-planetary commission and intelligently deciphered.

Only two successful Martian scout ship landings have occurred. One was at Sebastopol on Thursday, June 18th, 1959, at 11.2 a.m. G.M.T. and the other was at the Northern sector of Moscow on Sunday, October 4th, 1959, at 4.52 p.m. G.M.T. The latter ship was actually photographed, together with its complement of four Martians, by a Russian woman attached to the inter-planetary research department of the Russian Department of Technology, inter-planetary division."

It is evident that, if this information is accurate, we see the approaching end of the entire international espionage system! What proof in fact exists in this matter? Although there has been nothing in the form of official confirmation, we are entitled to draw certain conclusions from events which subsequently took place in the life of Richard Grave.

An account of Richard Grave's "directed" visit to Czechoslovakia in May, 1963, is to be found in Chapter 5 of this book. The relevant fact is that he entertained no reservations in making available to important Czechoslovak officials the entire story of his experience with the entity from another dimension and left with them samples of Universal Link literature including the particulars dictated to him in regard to the alleged Russian contact with the Martian scout craft. In May, 1967, four years after his first visit, Richard Grave returned on invitation to Czechoslovakia (at no financial cost to himself) and was flown by his Czechoslovak hosts to meet a group of interested Russians on Russian soil. The topic of discussion was the Universal Link and contact with extra-terrestrials. On his return to England Richard Grave said that the Russians discussed this subject in a matter of fact manner and expressed to him their view that sensitives on the Earth plane were being contacted by extra-terrestrials.

We may ask, would these visits by Richard Grave to Czechoslovakia and Russia have come about, and would Richard Grave have been treated with such courtesy and respect, if the information communicated to him in England about events stated to have taken place in Russia had not been significant and contained at least the substance of truth?

Recently the Russian biologist V.F. Kuprevich of the U.S.S.R. Academy of Sciences set forth a number of interesting ideas on life in outer space in the daily newspaper Sovetskaya Rossiya. Among them he poses the question: "Were the 'seeds' of life brought to Earth from outer space?" He claims that such a possibility cannot be excluded and goes on to reinforce the hypothesis of his colleague in the Soviet Academy of Sciences, Dr. I.S. Shklovsky (joint author with Harvard astronomer Dr. Carl Sagan of "Intelligent Life in the Universe") that the satellites of Mars are artificial and point to intelligent inhabitants existing, or having existed, on that planet.

Although there remains a wide gap between the readiness of a growing number of scientists to accept the possibility that some UFOs may be intelligently operated and extra-terrestrial in origin, and their readiness to accept that telepathic communication between extra-terrestrial intelligence and Earth man may already be an accomplished fact, reports of highly significant messages purporting to come from outer space or from other dimensions continue to reach us. We do not regard it as our function to analyse and evaluate the material on this subject which we publish for your information, but we are naturally selective in regard to it and it remains for the individual reader to attach his own sense of value to the information put before him.

The "Orlon" Messages

Messages conveying an assurance of hope, unspeakable joy and of grace outpoured continue, despite the depressing headlines in our newspapers, to flow in upon us. The consciousness of a growing number of sensitive individuals is being opened up to other dimensional intimations which appear to indicate that, irrespective of our deserts and of our evaluation of what we need, we are on the threshold of being offered help of a physical and not merely spiritual order as we move from the old age into the new.

Prominent among the reports reaching us is an account we have received from Denver, Colorado, U.S.A. Quite recently a sensitive, who is personally known to us and whom we will call Vesta, unexpectedly received a clear telepathic message from one who announced himself as a space being by the name of Orlon. The initial message came with great force and clarity but was so surprising in its content that Vesta went through a lengthy process of self-questioning and of "testing" the experience described in her report to us. While messages being given to other sensitives deal with the same theme, Vesta's messages have their own unique stamp and content.

First, Orlon seemed intent on emphasising that the purpose of initiating the contact was to establish a means of conveying information, as might be necessary from time to time, about "present plans being made for the evacuation of this planet." It was this initial message which particularly surprised Vesta who had not hitherto in any sense been thinking in these terms. A few days later, on 6th January, 1968, she questioned the original message and received telepathic confirmation of its accuracy. On the same day she received the following telepathic message from Truth (the entity associated with Richard Grave and the Universal Link who is now reportedly communicating to many individuals throughout the world):

"The work for which you are presently chosen is of deep import and great must be your faithfulness in its undertaking. The New Age bursts upon man with stunning suddenness and much stabilization is needed. What you are to do will consist in bringing balance measures to the attention of those alert enough to understand them and, with this, such information as is needful concerning the roles soon to be undertaken by those children of Light who fill your skies at present. The former will in many ways be new information. The latter will be more in the nature of reiteration of that which is presently being received by other channels. However, each reinforces the other, and each channel, due to the particular background involved, is capable of receiving more fully in certain areas than in others. In this way is the whole fabric woven and the interdependence of the threads is My chosen way of presenting the whole pattern. Receive and share! Receive and share! In these three words are summarized the motto of My New Age..."

Immediately after the foregoing message Orlon made contact and spoke as follows:

"I am here this morning to give you further information concerning our plans for this planet. It is quite understandable that you were startled by our first communication, and understandable that others also may be startled upon first hearing it. Nevertheless the message stands as it is.

It is true that peoples of Earth may soon expect to see us in large numbers as we carry out our mission for your planet. We of the Ashtar Command stand alert and ready for the action soon to come. We wait, as you do, the appointed moment, and may I say here that the appointed moment is as unknown to us as it is to you. We, too, are instructed to 'watch and wait.'

It is, however, known to us what the action is to be when the appointed moment comes. We stand poised on the brink of holocaust, ready to offer help to every being on your planet who will not resist our succour. This number will be small—infinitely small. Would it could be greater! And to increase that number is the greatest aim we have in using channels such as you. We ask your help in reaching as many contact points as possible."

The following day, 7th January, Vesta received from Truth this message: "That which you should know will be revealed to you. Do not ask questions now which a little trust and patience will show to be superfluous. Receiving is *receiving*, not a seeking to know, but a willingness to be told what is needful. It is an *in*flow, not a mind questing outwards. Sometimes you may well wonder why we do not always tell you certain things which could easily be revealed. Has it not occurred to you that this, too, is training in trust? The perfect channel lays soul open for the Father's imprint—hoping nothing, expecting nothing. Be thou My perfect channel. Do not ask. I shall tell you!"

On 8th January Orlon again made contact and spoke of "flying saucers" in the following remarkable terms:

"The 'saucers' which you speak of as such are in reality the space bodies of certain aggregates of consciousness. They exist duo-dimensionally: that is, they penetrate both the third and fourth dimensions simultaneously, or can, if they wish, confine themselves to either one of these. Their purpose has been, and still is, for the time being, to interlace these two realms of consciousness which are seemingly separate. However, the time quickly comes when the veil is torn aside and what *is* One is perceived as One. It is at this moment that the 'saucers' seen by the few will be seen by the many. It will appear that they have suddenly arrived in your skies in great number. In reality this is untrue. For in reality they are where they have always been, but man sees with new eyes."

Clarifying this further Orlon said that he was speaking of a metaphysical fact which would become more understandable as it was dwelt upon in meditation. He added, "By space body we mean the unified intent of the object as a whole, so that it behaves in every manner as if it were a single entity and functions as one intelligence. Those who fill it are individuals, true, but these individuals are so submitted to the Supreme Will that action takes place one-pointedly." He said that later he would go further into metaphysical facts.

On 9th January Orlon asked Vesta to record information that would be of help to all Light bearers. "This information," ran the message, "concerns the nature of atomic change within the body: information which, once understood, will make transformation easier. The cell structure within your bodies is so constituted that it is not permeable in the majority of cases to forces of Light-bearing quality. Only in relatively rare instances is the cell structure such that it *is* permeable and these cases you already know to be highly evolved souls who have offered their total beings to Light and have lived so pure a life that, quite literally, every cell is permeable. For the rest of you—I speak now of Light-bearers—your bodies are light in some areas, but in others they are, as yet, opaque. It goes without saying that these areas must be transmuted, so that to a certain degree you will experience in a minor way what the remainder of mankind must experience totally. The symptoms of change are, then, the same for all and each of you will experience it according to the level of your evolvement; that is, according to the areas which remain to be transmuted."

In the course of these transmissions Vesta on one occasion remarked upon the excessive tiredness felt not only by herself but also by others and

Orlon explained that the energies now flooding the earth were of such high frequency that most people could at first only respond to them intermittently. "After a response during which you feel lifted beyond your ordinary frequency you will find that an inevitable reaction occurs as a kind of balancing-out process. That is, old cells now vibrating at the new high pitch find a peak point beyond which they cannot respond and a cut-off spontaneously occurs after which they enter a period of non-response akin to resting, which you feel as tiredness." Orlon recommended almonds and oranges or orange juice (for easy assimilation of the almonds) be added to the diet and taken as a means for quick restoration of energy and requested Vesta to be patient both with herself and others who were going through this period of adjustment. He also explained that an emotional factor was here involved, since few were ready to experience a protracted state of joy without a reaction of flatness or "deadness" sometimes occurring. Soon, he assured her, the idea of "adjustment" in the mind would be replaced by "peace."

Soon after these transmissions began Truth made contact and defined Vesta's new work as receiving and disseminating to those ready to receive it "information concerning the efforts of certain interplanetary intelligences to help this Earth in its travail" and explained that such beings could not be of service in this cause without the help of "ground-wires."

On 10th January Orlon stated his desire to recapitulate the general information which was being given to other channels. This he did in the following terms:

> "The 'saucers' which have been sighted in your skies in increasing numbers for the past ten years are interplanetary attempts to bring your earth to balance. Great has been our difficulty in attempting to contact your people either personally or telepathically, due to forces present in your governments which would prevent this. Such forces would, if they had their way, bring total destruction to your planet. Our efforts have been attempts at counterbalancing, neutralizing the destructive elements and, wherever possible, raising the vibrations of man. Until or unless the thinking of man is elevated, disease, war and poverty will continue their deadly ravage. Today your world stands teetering on the brink of total disaster—closer, much closer than you dream. Like you, we can only stand by for the moment of decisive action when man's destructiveness pinpoints itself into a single gesture which would destroy a world. *Total negation calls forth total Light,* and the All Knowing One waits until all things are ready.

When Vesta asked what would be the nature of the external manifestation of Truth, Orlon replied: "GLORY!—the glory of Knowing, the glory of

Seeing, the glory of *total participation* in Truth!"

It may here be appropriate to refer back to a message given by Truth on Christmas Day to a widely known and loved sensitive living in Grand Rapids, Michigan, U.S.A. No doubt this message was designed to bring clarification to those who by their interpretation of the Universal Link Revelation were expecting an external manifestation of Truth around Christmas time. The message pointed out that the Revelation was interpreted according to the understanding of every individual and that this was inevitably how it had to be. "You can now understand," the message ran, "that without the element of suspense and the anticipation of some phenomenal demonstration my mission could not have been achieved, for it was this sense of expectancy which caught the imagination of my children all over the world and made them open and receptive to my Light and my Vibration. Thus has my Universal Chain been forged and all my Light Centres have merged into ONE mighty force of Power and Light and none can ever return to their old state of inertness and lethargy..." We do not intend to augment the discussions which have been taking place since then as to whether and in what manner the prophecies in relation to the Universal Link Revelation were fulfilled beyond saying that Truth has consistently affirmed through many different channels, as have also a great many individuals in their own reported experiences, that the prophecy, taken as applying to a great cosmic release of high frequency energies, was fulfilled in a variety of manifestations affecting the spiritual lives of great numbers of individuals. It is evident that some specific event or events are—at a date and hour no man can tell—yet to take place. The principal happening is, according to messages being channelled through sensitives widely dispersed throughout the world, to be connected with energies quite suddenly released by man himself, and after this event life will everywhere be very different.

With regard to the time factor Orlon pertinently remarks: "To wonder is human, but to lead your lives in such a manner that the hour matters *not* is Divine. Let your *Divinity* shine!" He also gave Vesta the following information which many will find interesting in the light of references to this same subject which appear in messages from other sensitives at this time:

> "You are wondering, many of you, whether you will be 'taken' or remain. Let us clarify this matter. Those who remain will be those who are so stabilized in every aspect of their being that their own heat-energy will generate their warmth. These are, most generally, those who have purified their bodies to such a degree that every cell will accomplish transmutation with (comparative) ease. For the rest of you, who have purified yourselves in other aspects, but whose bodies are not yet clarified, help of an extra-terrestrial nature will be provided. You will *all* be helped, let me

make that clear, but for some a temporary *removal and renewal* will be necessary. Let us also make it clear that there is *no* 'higher' or 'lower' among those who go or stay: it is simply a matter of rendering each one fit for the great task ahead in the fastest possible manner. Those who stay will also be given personal assistance, but this will be of a different nature than the help given those who are taken. Separation within families will in most cases be inevitable, but so great will be the wonderment of all of you, the *joy* and wonderment, that it will not seem to be separation at all. For all of you it will be a graduation from the personal family relationships you have always known—into the great Family of God."

It is impossible not to be struck by the note of immediacy which characterizes so many of the inspirational and telepathic messages being given us today, and although we are continually being reminded of the need for attunement to love and higher wisdom as the proper ever-prevailing state of our consciousness, irrespective of outer level happenings, there is the undeniable pointer in a great many of these messages to some very special event which is to happen suddenly and soon. Our final quotation from Orlon will be his exhortation to all Light-bearers in anticipation of this event:

"Please convey to other Light-bearers the red alert sign—the flashing red alert—that they may be on hand for coming climactic events.

Events upon your planet begin to reach zero hour. Let each of you be ready on a moment's notice to drop whatever you are doing to follow the Father's guidance. Peace and calm are the watchwords. Stay immersed in these and you will indeed be ready! As we have said many times, it is not what you *accomplish* which helps us most *but the prevailing attitude of your mind.* We need, right now, all the co-operation you and others can give, and that co-operation is the constant flowing outward of Peace and Light and Love. All else will be told you, but see that you remain in a condition *to* be told! When you lie down to sleep, put yourself in a state of awareness of Love. Think Love, feel Love, send Love out to others. Think of your Earth as enfolded with the Total Light and Love of God. Think of that Light and Love penetrating deep into soil of earth, drenching and filling to overflowing the saddened hearts of men. Play with the idea of Love, and let your imagination soar! Then sleep. If you do this you open pathways, even in sleep, into the dark places where Light and Love have never been. But you do more than this. You also put *yourself* into that rate of vibration where we can work with and expand your knowing, like threads cast out on which strong ropes are built. We ask of you filaments only; and delicate and fragile as they may seem to you, with what astonishment would you observe the ladders built from them!

Give Love and you will be absorbed in Love. *Think* Love and Love will think its own right action through you. He who blesses is most blessed of all."

The "Gildas" Teachings

In this section we wish to draw attention to other material which has come into our hands and which we consider to be of exceptional importance in relation to the coming changes. This material, so far as we have been able to discover, is unique in the detailed references it provides regarding the conditions which mankind may expect to experience after certain radical happenings have taken place. While we are grateful for permission to quote from among the more informative passages in these teachings, a word of introduction in regard to the group from which they stem would seem to be appropriate.

The group in question has no specific territorial base but includes readers scattered over Britain, linked mainly by letters. Application for these teachings may be made in writing to the secretary, Miss Mary Swainson, 77 Wigston Road, Oadby, Leicester, LE2 5QG, England. (Please do not telephone or visit.) Initially a donation should be sent to cover cost of literature and postage.

The source of these teachings is the "guide," or an aspect of the "higher self" of a young woman who has been carefully prepared over many years on a firm basis of considerable psychological and spiritual groundwork. There is no question of trance nor of automatic writing; communication is by direct use of developed and trained higher faculties—an art which, through aspiration, discrimination and constant practice will become more widespread as man develops his sixth and further senses in the new age. In estimating the value of the messages, however, their origin and the manner of their communication, although interesting, are of secondary importance. The prime consideration is the saying: "By their fruits ye shall know them," so it is hoped that readers will use their individual discernment to find whether or not the following examples of the work "speak to their condition."

We have been quoting from the work of sensitives in the U.S.A. and it is interesting to note how the remarks of Gildas accord with and implement the observations about the time factor in relation to the "moment of change." In one of his communications Gildas speaks about this question in these words:

"There must be much wondering, among those who are spiritually awakened to awareness of the 'other side,' about the new age and the new developments which have been promised. You must be patient. Why are you so worried about exact timing? If only we could teach you to worry less about time; you are always asking 'when?' or 'how soon?' Is it not enough for you that these things are *going* to happen? They have been promised and you have the privilege of helping to prepare for them. There is a danger which I think you have glimpsed of living in the future; you must learn to use the present; do not let it pass you by; learn to attune yourselves more each day to the 'other worlds.' We are relying on you who have seen something, be it only a glimpse, of what can take place when the two worlds approach each other and easy interchange can take place. Much of our work can be done only through you. Do not merely look forward to the future, but concentrate on opening yourselves in the present to be channels of receptivity."

On another occasion Gildas speaks about the need for preparation as follows:

"Preparation is indeed necessary, but it is a preparation in tranquillity and relaxation which you seem to be needing most now. A relaxed mind is an open mind; you also need to achieve far less emphasis in the area of the mind, much more in the area of the heart.

These changes of which we speak will bring the utmost beauty, peace and contentment, and you must educate your bodies to the right degree of harmony that you may receive the greater blessing, the truer contact... Your great task of preparation is to become islands of tranquillity in the midst of a busy and anxious world. The more you can achieve this even in a lesser degree, the easier it will be to effect a smooth contact when the time for the 'changes' is here.

You fear that the 'changes' should bring about destruction, pain and chaos and you have heard from many sides of this possibility. This may be to some extent true, but we are working towards a state where pain and destruction would be minimal. You must surely know that we would never plan purposely to bring hurt and degradation on a mass scale in this way. Yet, however it may be, you must learn to trust that that which will grow from the change will quickly heal all the hurt which may have been caused and any disturbance of this kind will melt into a blessed forgetfulness. In the age of gold, man will remember but not relive his pain and the remembrance shall be tempered with understanding and thankfulness and will only serve to show forth the blessedness of the true communion which shall be known.

The pain and destruction will only be necessary if we cannot find a certain degree of harmony. To bring about changes such as these to a world which is materialistic, dark and grasping will inevitably cause pain and destruction because of the sudden contrast—the sudden explosion which would occur as vibrations are raised to the heights to which they *will* be raised. Therefore we teach those who are aware to practise harmony, that they may be used as links in the new circuit, and the shock to the world will be as brief and mild as possible. The power is immense and strong, and these changes will take very careful handling indeed if they are to come with the smoothness which is possible if the conditions are right. That is why we rely on you so much. This is why last year I asked that you should take every opportunity of helping to prepare men's hearts and minds for this great age in every way that is possible. Even the minutest degree of awareness in one individual when added to that in another will show forth an effect and make for greater harmony in all that is to come... To learn to practise this harmony you must begin in the most humble spheres, bringing it right down into everything, even the most trivial task. Learn to make harmonious movements, endeavour to shut out from your lives as much as possible all sudden noises, consider your nervous system in the minutest ways. Every disharmony, no matter how small, adds up and spoils the whole. Think of your lives as a prayer and an offering upon the altar of Light and strive to make each thing you do worthy in harmony to take place within the temple of Light.

The time of loneliness will soon be over, the painful preparations will not have to be re-lived; you will be clean, pure and receptive and when the changes come will be filled immediately with pure light, so that you may turn and help with joy those who will then come to you with open and receptive hearts."

One day in answer to a question Gildas spoke as follows:

"The second sun which you see as making nonsense of all the imagery which includes the sun as centre of the universe, we see not so much as an actual second sun but as man's second sight of all that is now...this is the extra dimension again. This world and what is so often called the other world will intermingle and you will see all in a glorious new light, as *though* from a second sun, so that in imagery you may say that a second sun will enter into the lives, the hearts, the universe of mankind as it is now.

On one occasion Gildas gave an exemplary reply to someone in the group who inquired about his views in regard to messages some groups were receiving to the effect that they would be told when to assemble to be "taken off in a flying saucer." Gildas replied: "There are different degrees of understanding and everyone must do what he has to do. Our duty lies in doing what we have to do and allowing others to do what they have to do."

In the autumn of 1967 Gildas spoke about the inner significance of relationships and of group meetings in the following words:

"You may wonder at the pattern behind everything you often try too actively to plan and organize and arrange. All is taken care of; you need only to cultivate quiet yet open minds and hearts and to learn to put your trust completely in those who would lovingly guide you. You cannot see the ways in which the contacts you make are used, yet once a true contact *is* made, then it continues always to grow and to deepen, whether you remain physically close to one another or not. From this side we make great use of all your meetings, all your meditations. Through you and in you we send out light and power to all the world, and when you work in groups, in depth, in co-operation, then the focusing point for all the power is strengthened and multiplied far beyond the normal laws of number or physics. Do not then plan too actively; do not seek to structure relationships but rather live tranquilly from the still centre, yet taking every opportunity that may be offered to try yourselves in the light of another's belief and understanding, and thus to make stronger the great forces that work for the Light in all that is to come...

You have to get rid of the feeling that 'impersonal' necessarily means 'cold' and to understand it in this context as meaning getting beyond the ego, loving with the whole being (i.e. including the ego and beyond it), including the higher self and the deep centre and learning to put the desires of the ego on to a secondary level to the creating of a fulfilled relationship. It is a gradual process and often a painful one, each stage of the lesson being learned through the mistakes the ego makes."

We shall be concluding this chapter with a precis of a summary which Gildas himself has given of his teachings and information communicated to the group over a period of several months. First, however, we would like to share with you the following precis of our human condition and the coming changes as specially prepared for inclusion in this chapter by the "Principal" of an "agent" who is a member of the group:

"There is much speculation in the world today regarding various types of cataclysmic events, the Second Coming and the New

Age. We would like to see if we can clarify the situation a little.

At the moment the world is in a difficult stage of transition as she moves from the Piscean age to that of Aquarius. The 'changes' referred to by many people are all directly associated with this fact. The situation today is not unlike that of a woman in labour, only the whole of mankind is involved in the birth of the New Age. Some revel in this, others are frightened; some are supremely excited and are prepared to participate in full consciousness, while others prefer a state of anaesthesia where they neither feel nor think.

The changes which are taking place are raising the earth's vibrations; this will enable man, provided he is 'awake' and 'aware,' to raise his own understanding from the limitations of three dimensional (five sense) existence to a four dimensional (six or more sense) existence. There are a number of people who are already aware that changes are taking place and they are working hard to benefit from this and to learn the lessons which it is now possible to experience. One of the most important of these lessons which man should strive to practise is right thinking—positive, creative thought is an essential of the New Age where thought will become as real as solid matter is today. In order therefore to avoid chaos, not only must thought be positive and clear, but rightly orientated to God's Laws and not to the will of man. Those who realize the truth of this statement know that this is a practical proposition and that the act of manipulating thought energy produces results which seem incredible by normal material standards.

Mankind, or some men, while expecting a changed state on Earth are also expecting a Second Coming. The return of the Christ will first be an individual and *internal* event for each person. The changes in the world will help to lead man to this supreme experience, but there will not be one 'external medium' for the Christ in the New Age. In the early stages, however, when but a few receive this revelation, they may be heralded by their associates as new Messiahs. The New Age is sometimes referred to as the Golden Age. This is what it will become when all men have experienced their individual adult Christening.

There is a great deal of work to be done in order to ensure that at the final moment of change, of birth, there are enough men ready to proceed with the building of the New Age. Some realize already that it has begun to emerge, others will slowly begin to awaken to this fact, but the vast majority of mankind is still sound asleep and does not realize that the age of materialism must die and give way to the new. There will therefore be a climax to the birth pangs which will catapult man into this realization; a shock will be given to mankind by man himself. The exact nature of this climax cannot be explained nor can the time be predicted.

There is therefore a dual situation: on the one hand the strivings of mankind as he experiences the birth of the New Age and works to assist in its arrival and on the other hand the individual internal search for the birth of the Christ within. The first, which is a cosmic event, will proceed in spite of man, while the latter will only materialise when each man himself has earned the right to revelation. The two events may be said to be complementary for eventually they will form an interwoven whole. The climax to these two 'births' will, however, only occur simultaneously for a very few.

Health, Holiness and Happiness are the birthright of the New Age. To achieve the right to claim this for himself mankind must re-orientate himself to God's Will. The surest way to set out on this journey is to begin by learning to think only those thoughts which, were they to materialize, man would be proud and happy for the world to see. The New Age will come as surely as night follows day, but it will only be a Golden Age when it can reflect this gold from the hearts of all men."

Finally, the following is a precis of a remarkable reply given by Gildas to various questions which had been raised over a period of time by members of the group and which Gildas answered comprehensively in October, 1967:

"We understand your anxieties about the changes of which we speak and the desire for more specific knowledge of all that is to happen. We must warn you that now you are blind in comparison with what you will be after these events. You are bound in an entangled web compounded of physical limitations and over-concern with matter and time. We do not say that it is your *fault*, but it is your *condition*, and by it your understanding is bound and limited.

We will talk to you as specifically as possible about the changes and what they will involve. You must expect that not all will be pleasant and you must endeavour to look beyond that which you may find frightening or dreadful to the assurances we give, that the final outcome shall be joy and blessing unlimited. Initially for many, however, all that has long been of prime importance in their lives will disappear and the changes will have an enormous impact in many fields.

Man's destiny is, as it has ever been, in his own hands, and it is not from 'above' or from another plane that the great explosion which will precipitate the changes shall be initiated. In a small moment of time someone on Earth will unleash a great energy, and not until the moment when the irrevocable decision is made will it be realized how fractional is man's comprehension of energy of this kind. The initial changes will be over in moments and it is for this reason that we speak to you in such terms as cataclysm and holocaust. *Be assured that wonder and joy shall eventually be seen as the result.* There will, however, be a time of trial and suffering for all except those whose hearts and minds are prepared.

For a while after the initial and cataclysmic happenings there will be a period of adjustment to lessen the suffering and to enable those who are prepared in advance to realize the full and glorious potential of all that has been brought about, and the work of these shall be fulfilling and joyful.

Because of the greatly increased vibrations your very bodies will undergo change and their material needs will be considerably less. There will therefore be no need to plan minutely about such things as you now consider to be essential services. It may sound utopian, but all you have need of will be provided. You will enter immediately into new fields of knowledge and experience and will know at the moment these events take place what to do.

For too long man has developed the wrong centres of the brain, relying too much upon the physical, upon matter, and neglecting his spirit and soul. He has concentrated upon the wonder of only five of his senses.

The true power of thought shall come into its own and, as this power is generally recognized and explored, man will think with humour of the complications of the ingenious but clumsy and energy-consuming methods which are now so often his pride. When your minds are suitably developed and you become aware of other brain centres, then you will be able to accept even more subtle experiences on ever higher vibrational levels. So you progress, when the time is right, to a more subtle body and a higher plane. There you will learn what experience on that plane can teach you, and so the soul will progress ever higher until it attains mastery and everlasting communion with the Ultimate.

Disease, weariness, all the things that worry you now, will no longer be. That which you cannot heal yourselves in the light of your new knowledge will instantly be adjusted by those above, who will guide you with love. Thus you will hardly be aware of any illness or any state that is other than perfect. But there is another side to this: whereas many of you will feel free and exhilarated, there will be others—in fact a large majority—who will experience a great sense of shock. All that they now recognize as 'life' and 'worth living for' will be wiped out at one stroke. Yet the minds of many will be open, and their hearts ready, and it will be the task of those who, because of their preparation, will enter instantly into the higher knowledge, to teach, heal and to feed spiritually the masses who need help. This will be a work of joy and love. Many wonderful things will happen. The centres of love in man shall be activated at a very high level and there will be peace and understanding all over the earth."

Chapter Seven

Between the years 1961 and 1967 an archetypal Christ-like being, apparently in solid form, made frequent appearances to Richard Grave in England (and subsequently, as reported, to persons elsewhere) and announced in a series of dictated statements that a universal cosmic operation was in progress ushering in the New Age.

Throughout these years, in newsletters and statements released throughout the world, the one appearing to Richard became known as Truth, Limitless Love or the All Knowing One. He spoke in the first person singular in the name of the Lord, after the manner of prophets and angels in the scriptures, and claimed to be imparting information about the way God is operating in the universe at this time.

His most crucial statement was that by Christmas, 1967, he would have revealed himself to the universe "through the medium of nuclear evolution." He also spoke of a build-up of international tension towards a major world conflict. A human press-button device would be used and, simultaneously with the pressing of the button, instead of disaster the Universal Revelation would occur. He also said: "To effect My Materialization I require many instruments and this will create, to an extent, confusion." A link-up has been effected throughout all continents and a great many countries between a substantial number of individuals and groups of individuals. But when he spoke of "My Universal Direct Link" he was primarily referring, at least in my own understanding, to the new possibilities being given, through transforming energies now being released, of the establishment or restoration of direct contact between God and individual man. Throughout these years, and especially towards the close of 1967, an ever increasing number of individuals reported having transforming spiritual experiences and a deepening of their sense of universal love to a degree and extent that left them fully satisfied with regard to the claim that the revelation had taken place.

Others, however, expected outward events which manifestly have not as yet taken place. Some have pointed out that, by a seeming coincidence, China attempted to conduct a large nuclear explosion in a test which took place on 24th December. The Atomic Energy Commission subsequently confirmed that the device contained all the ingredients of a thermonuclear explosion but the small explosive force of the detonation indicated that the thermonuclear material did not ignite. There are some who have pointed out that this event may, in the context of the revelation, have at least a symbolic significance as a token of an explosion of energy of greater force which is yet to occur and which will have altogether unexpected results.

Meanwhile, however, we have to take into account the appearance of Truth to Richard Grave on 31st December, 1967, and his statement: "My Universal Revelation through the medium of nuclear evolution is complete... I have revealed Myself fully as promised. The whole of nuclear energy is Me and My whole power completely under My control." But in the same statement he goes on to refer to an event apparently still in the future: "Remember, I will come with suddenness and in the next second. The universal love flow is increasing. All is well."

At this point, can we dismiss the entire revelation? This would not be easy. What, then, are we being told? Are we to infer that from the end of 1967 more and more individuals will be able to link more readily with the transforming energies of the Christos? There is certainly encouraging evidence, from reports being received, that some new enabling force is more operative, as it were, in our midst. Although to our rational and scientific understanding one hesitates to speak of a new energy, we are forcibly reminded of the prophecy given from a mystical experience by that great master of Light, Sri Aurobindo, in 1931. At that time he was speaking of a "new Force" and a "descending Light" to which he gave the name "Supra-mental." He claimed that this force was already exerting itself on the consciousness of man and that it would "enter a phase of realizing power by 1967." In the same breath he was speaking of "a new kind of theocracy, the Kingdom of God upon earth, a theocracy which shall be the government of mankind by the Divine in the hearts and minds of men."

Perhaps we are still rather too close to 1967 to know what has happened, and we shall only know fully in retrospect as events in the consciousness of man and in the outer world take their course. It seems that we shall indeed need a special saving grace and all the empowerment and understanding God can give us to enable us to meet and overcome the challenges of the present time.

Meanwhile, there is at least one tremendous event which took place in 1967 of the highest symbolic significance for the times in which we live. The huge import of this was brought home to me by a radio talk given in England by the Chief Rabbi of the British Commonwealth on the eve of Good Friday. He pointed out that the real significance of the sensational events of June, 1967, when the Jews regained control of Jerusalem, lay in their link with the opening verses of the First Chapter of the Acts of the Apostles which deals with the exchanges which took place between Jesus and the apostles immediately prior to his Ascension. Jesus referred to his promise to send the Spirit of Truth to them, telling them to wait in Jerusalem until the promise had been fulfilled (Pentecost took place 40 days later). They thereupon asked him if this would be the time when the sovereignty of Israel would be restored. Jesus replied that this knowledge was the prerogative of God himself and he was then "taken up: and a cloud received him out of their sight." We are reminded that after the death of King Herod (about 1 A.D.) the Romans seized the opportunity to extend their sovereignty over the whole of the area which later became known as Palestine which included, of course, Jerusalem itself. Israel recovered the sovereignty of Jerusalem for the first time since that date in the year 1967.

While on the subject of the Ascension of Jesus, one of the major Biblical incidents which seems so strangely irrational to the modern mind, it is of some interest to observe the direction in which the search for rational explanations is leading us. There are today scientists, both in the East and in the West, who claim that there is evidence to indicate that in times past the earth has been visited by intelligent beings from other planets, but who would have believed we would reach the day when a Soviet scientist would seriously offer the theory that a space ship take-off may have given rise to the story of the Ascension? Yet this is precisely the theory put forward by a scientist, Dr. E. Fyoderov, in an article printed recently in Krasnaya Zvezda, the newspaper of the Soviet Ministry of Defence. Dr. Fyoderov in his article criticizes those who scoff at suggestions that the earth may have been visited by inhabitants of other planets and points out that not even the sceptics deny the likelihood that advanced civilizations have arisen on other planets. "Therefore," he concludes, "it is logical to assume that among a large number of civilizations there are some that have conducted broad explorations in space and it is possible that the explorers were in the region of the earth before life arose in the form that we know it." Although no direct evidence may have been found, Dr. Fyoderov points out that indirect evidence exists in myths and legends and cites the Ascension of Jesus Christ as one such example. "Can we not," he says, "theorize that this 'fact' originated when a visiting spaceship took aboard someone from earth? And don't the circumstances of the destruction of the cities of Sodom and Gomorrah suggest nuclear explosions?" I have no intention of adding to the speculation raised by these queries, but it will certainly do no harm for us to think more deeply about these things for ourselves and reach our own conclusions about any relevance they may have for us in these days. It would be easy, though it might not be wise, to dismiss such theories out of hand and before I leave this subject, which I think is likely to impinge more, rather than less, on the consciousness of man in the days ahead, I would like to draw your attention to a biological and scientific study of this subject in a book called "Uninvited Visitors" by Ivan T. Sanderson (Cowles Education Corporation, 488 Madison Avenue, New York, N.Y., 10022, USA—$6.95). Writing about the origin of man Mr. Sanderson raises questions which challenge the popular conception that man is indigenous to this planet and an end-product of evolution upon it and that there is nothing in the geological record to show that the process has been tampered with from outside. He points out that many throughout the centuries have claimed otherwise and that we need seriously to consider the possibility that our planet has been visited by superior intelligences throughout its history and also quite recently.

May we for the moment leave the last word on this subject to the eminent psychologist, the late Carl Gustav Jung? When the controversy over the subject of flying saucers was at its height and a disturbing number of sightings were being reported over a wide area of the world, Dr. Jung was serving as Chief Psychologist for the Aerial Phenomena Research Organization in Alamogordo, New Mexico. In an internationally circulated newspaper Dr. Jung was reported as saying: "UFO phenomena are not mere rumour. A purely psychological explanation is ruled out by the fact that a large number of observations have proven inexplicable as natural phenomena." He added that credibility of the existence of UFOs had been given by the fact that the U.S.A. and Canada had set up bureaux to compile reports on them. In the interview he said: "These discs do not behave in accordance with physical laws but as though they were without weight. They show evidence of intelligent guidance by quasi-human pilots for their accelerations are such that no normal humans can survive." Dr. Jung added: "Should the extra-terrestrial origin of the UFOs be proven, it might have the same effect on the human race that the superior technology of western Europe had on primitive cultures. Just as the Pax Brittanica put an end to the disputes between the tribes of Africa, so our world could unroll its Iron Curtain and use it as scrap iron with all the millions of tons of guns, warships and munitions." This carefully worded statement calls to mind the way Lenin is reliably reported to have expressed himself during a conversation in 1920 with Mr. H.G. Wells, the eminent historian and writer of science fiction, when he said: "All human conceptions are on the scale of our planet... If we succeed in establishing interplanetary communications all our philosophical, moral and social views will have to be revised. In this case the technical potential, become limitless, would impose the end of the rule of violence as a means and method of progress."

Alas! Dr. Jung in regard to this subject is better known for his subsequent recantation as the result of the hornet's nest of criticism, abuse and ridicule to which these earlier remarks from a man of such high professional standing in the world gave rise. In a sudden shift of view he began calling UFOs the result of "the world's psychological need of fantasy," and in effect dismissed the entire subject in a single sentence, saying that the minds of those who observed these things "are cornered by the bad situation in which the world is today. They are in need of answers to their anxious questions which nobody can give them. That is why they let their fantasy run on the lines of flying saucers and similar objects." It seems almost as if someone sharply reminded him that his high standing in the world was *as a psychologist* and that it would be advisable for him to express his thoughts on the subject in a purely psychological framework.

My reason for writing somewhat lengthily on this subject is because a number of scientists today, in Russia as well as in the West, are proclaiming the whole UFO question as the greatest scientific problem of our time, and not long ago U Thant, the Secretary General of the United Nations, had the courage to declare himself to be in line with this view and was roundly castigated in the leading article of an influential American daily newspaper for so expressing himself. It remains to be seen what is to be revealed to the world by the publication of the Condon Commission, at present conducting the Colorado University Investigation. Because of the high scientific reputation of the University of Colorado the report is awaited with widespread interest, but it is already known that the views of the members of the Commission are sharply divided and that two of its members have broken away and will be producing their own minority report.*

Meanwhile telepathic intimations are not lacking that at some time in the not too distant future the peoples of our planet might quite suddenly see spacecraft in great numbers in the skies above. One can imagine the psychic shock in store for those who have firmly set their minds against the possibility of such a vision and so it seems wise at least to keep an open mind in regard to the sightings, touch-down landings and even encounters with beings of other realms and dimensions which continue to be reported from different parts of the world.

Today the view is being expressed by many people that in some indefinable way the flow of energy circulating in the world and through the structure of our very beings seems to have been greatly increased. We talk about the population explosion and the technological explosion and we note the way energy is apparently running loose in the more acute forms in which rioting and revolts in one form or another are an almost daily occurrence in many countries. It is as if rational living has acted in such a way as to hamper the full flow of expression of the transforming energy which now more than ever seems to be pressing in upon us and that if we are unable to make use of it for transformation it will find its expression in disruptive ways. Some claim that we are being irradiated more powerfully from the universe itself and ask whether the tremendous energies emanating from the quasars (quasi-stellar radio sources), which continue to mystify the scientists, may in some way have a bearing on our manifestly overall disturbed condition. And now we are told by scientists in Russia and in the United States that 1968 is "The Year of the Troubled Sun," when the surface of the sun will erupt in storms of violent activity, following a well defined cycle. Every eleven years there is a short period of activity, but there are also periods of longer and more intense solar "storms" at intervals of 80 and 400 years. These three phases of activity have

The material in this chapter was written in 1968.

been astronomically calculated all to occur together in 1968. We are to expect the possibility of streams of radiation greater than any previously experienced.

Some of our psychologists, too, are making interesting observations. They acknowledge the growing and widespread sense and conviction that something is about to burst. It might, of course, be in what we call the external world or it could be the sense of something coming to bursting point within ourselves, which is seen as foreshadowing an event as crucial as anything that could occur in the external world. The pressures are everywhere building up on a wide front and it is common knowledge that people young and old are by various means looking for a way of escape out of a world which seems too small or too inadequate and distasteful to them. Others, as individuals and in widely scattered groups, are in their own lives and activities already laying the foundations of a new world and a new and universal civilization. I will return to this later in the chapter.

Now I want to turn from this picture of our overall human condition to the challenge it presents to each one of us here and now. It would be misleading for any responsible individual to imagine, and still less publicly to proclaim, that the immediate future for the general run of humanity will be all sweetness and light. We can say with certainty that there is plenty of trouble in store for mankind in the future. Yet we need to bear in mind that we can be of least help to the human situation, or to ourselves, by becoming emotionally or actively involved in the confusion around us. This is not to say that we shall not find ourselves acting in any situation in a way that is true to ourselves and to our understanding, and from the springs of compassion and love which the impingement of the troubles of mankind arouse deep within us. But nothing is more important at this hour than that we should continually be mindful of our true spiritual identity. There is a level at which we can say that the spiritualization of the material world is in progress and reaching a climax: that all true work is work for the Coming of the Kingdom, for the Manifestation of the Divine on earth, for what Pierre Teilhard de Chardin calls the Christification of Man and the divinization of the world. Let us therefore be conscious that we constitute living cells in the Body of Christ, by whatever name throughout the universe this may be known—the One Unified Body. This is our true state of being if we acknowledge and are conscious of it. In this state of being and consciousness we are immortal here and now. We may remind ourselves that what we need is an enormous aspiration to manifest the highest we can conceive in terms of a quality of life and to remember that the "after life" world is not some world in the future. It is present now. Through the One Unified Body we shall know the New Heaven and build the New Earth. At the same time we may hold in mind the truth that in the tiniest particles of the universe, as also in the very big, which we call galaxies, reality consists largely of radiant light energy and we are one substance with all of this and are therefore lighthouses. The effectiveness of our radiant light, as also the experience of our eternal immortality, depends on our consciousness of this truth and the quality of our aspiration. There is a level at which it is true to say that the Divine Plan is not only pre-determined but is already fulfilled and that in the realization of this glorious fact we may feel uplifted and maintained in a state of continuous praise and rejoicing. But this is a mystical truth which our minds cannot readily assimilate. We are, however, conscious that the most potent of all light and love radiations are at the very core of the atom and that mention we have heard of revelation through nuclear evolution may embrace the explosive release of this tremendous radiant energy throughout the universe.

It may be true, as one inspired sensitive has expressed it, that a world of chaos and mighty turbulence in racial, cultural, physical and economic elements brings suffering and misunderstanding to those who see *only* with the outer eye and hear *only* with the outer ear, but "those who see and hear with inner awareness will perceive that My Plan can be fulfilled only when the outer has crumbled and fallen because it was built upon insecure foundations and of corruptible material out of the material-mindedness of man and that it could not survive. A world of lasting peace can come only when man sees himself and his brother with the light of Spirit and thinks of himself and others as spiritual beings who live and progress eternally by the images which they hold in their consciousness. You are the creator of all that comes to you. Bless My Light bearers who are able to see beyond the chaos and realize that only good will prevail. This does not mean that you may not experience the worldly unrest and the social and economic upheaval which prevail, but as you view it all from the spiritual level you can see that when this era is finished a new day of love and peace and understanding will come to pass."

The great majority of the inspired messages pouring through the consciousness of sensitive individuals throughout the world at this time dwells upon the changes due, if we may express it in astrological terms, to the shift from the Piscean to the Aquarian Age and to the increase in the rate of the earth's and of our own vibrations as we are raised to new levels of sensitivity, receptivity and awareness. It is in resistance to this process that we find the cause of so much of the confusion and suffering we see around us. In the immediate future we cannot expect this to diminish, but we can be sure of the strength, the power, the wisdom and the love upon which we can draw from moment to moment to enable us to master and rise beyond *any* situation which may challenge us. In our realization of the explosion of Light and Love which is potential in the core of every atomic particle of which we are composed, let us see ourselves as Light bearers, as Lighthouses radiating Love and Light to the furthest corners of the universe, for it is timely now for many of us to give somewhat less attention to *teachings* and to find ourselves engaged rather more continually in awareness of *being* and of radiating Light. The process taking place has recently been described in an inspired message in the following words:

"All the time you are being prepared for those days ahead when the darkness has passed away and the glorious light shall once more shine forth in all its power and glory. You are to hold before you in your consciousness the time of reconstruction, never of destruction. Every group working for the Light has a specific work which it is being prepared for, therefore it is very necessary that you each seek until you find what work is yours and, when you have found it, hold on to the vision I give you of it and let nothing pull you off or distort that vision. I want you even now to build for the glorious future, for the New Age. You are not to become involved in any way with the chaos and confusion and destruction which is to take place during the cleansing which is essential at this time, for if you were to become involved you would not be ready to do the work for which I have been preparing you through the ages; for when the old has been destroyed the New must be brought forth and you are to help bring forth the New."

We cannot tell what will ensue as mankind breaks the bonds of his five-sense, three-dimensional existence into a four-dimensional, new and more expansive environment with six or more senses in active operation, but as in the stillness of our meditation we focus upon the Light of the Cosmic Christ Body, of which we are each a living, vibrant cell, and upon his Universal Mission, to which we pledge ourselves anew, let me conclude with these words, in which I trust we may all find truth, guidance and a vision to strengthen and uphold us in the days to come:

"There is a wave of disturbance, a spiritual volcano, about to discharge itself on your earth. Be not dismayed; unrest and energy only prove that inherent life is at work. God's wheels must not clog. By all the wars and signs of the times, know that the Day of the Lord is at hand, your own Lord and Christ, the indwelling potent Christ of God. The keys of the Kingdom are in your hands. Out of chaos and confusion there will come peace and order to your earth. The wars of the nations are the birth pangs of a new era, and the consciousness of the race will be lifted by the pain and agony of the refiner's fire. In the hearts of those who have attained the Christ consciousness there will be rest and glorious hope, for they shall see the new dawn arising when Christ who is our Light shall reign."

Chapter Eight

The Great Invocation

From the point of Light within the Mind of God
Let light stream forth into the minds of men.
Let Light descend on Earth.

From the point of Love within the Heart of God
Let love stream forth into the hearts of men.
May Christ return to Earth.

From the centre where the Will of God is known
Let purpose guide the little wills of men —
The purpose which the Masters know and serve.

From the centre which we call the race of men
Let the Plan of Love and Light work out
And may it seal the door where evil dwells.

Let Light and Love and Power restore the Plan on Earth.

The title chosen for this chapter presupposes that there *is* an intelligently controlled and guided operation taking place throughout the universe; that by paying heed to revelation available to us we can achieve a significant insight into the nature of this vast and exceedingly complex operation; and that by a life of prayer, meditation and devotion we can discover the role which we are individually called upon to play in the operation which, so far as our planet is concerned, involves the long delayed restoration or perfecting of the earth as being essential to the fulfilment of the plan for cosmic restoration.

The word God, as it appears in the Great Invocation and elsewhere in this book, is universally intelligible even though not perhaps universally acceptable. However, giving it both an immanent and transcendent meaning, we are using it in preference to various possible alternatives among which, in some sections of society—especially in the communist parts of the world—is nowadays to be heard the expression "higher intelligence" (with which man is capable of making contact), in recognition of the fact that the intelligence of *homo sapiens* is not supreme throughout the universe. With our limited minds it is manifestly impossible to be very much aware of the nature of an intelligence greater than our own, and this is no doubt the reason why we have always been disposed to deify the great spiritual masters and angelic messengers who have come into our midst from time to time, and who are with us today to involve us by their teaching and example in the work of universal restoration.

What do we mean in simple terms by this reference to world and cosmic restoration? Among the peoples of all continents can be found traces of the universal myth which in the language of the Judaeo-Christian scriptures takes form in the story of Genesis of the creation of man, his loss of contact with God through his misuse of the gift of free will and of the consequences, which continue to this day, of man's individual and collective failure to respond to God's loving concern that he should consciously and freely realign his own will with the Will of his Creator and manifest in his environment upon the earth the conditions of perfection for which man and the world over which he was to have dominion were originally created. There is nothing revealed by science nor in the discoveries relating to man's biological and psychological evolution which disproves what the universal myth basically affirms, and now as ever man is from moment to moment free to choose whether to align his will with the Will of God—with the immutable and universal laws governing all creation—or to go his own way with laws of his own making. The entirety of human history has been the continuous story of God, as it were, reaching out to man in Love through a succession of patriarchs, prophets, kings, angelic messengers and spiritual emissaries, with the sole object of reminding man of his divine origin and that his individual and collective happiness depends upon a life lived in accordance with certain preordained laws. There may be more sophisticated ways of describing this long historical process, which many choose to see as the story of man's conscious evolution through the acquisition of knowledge and experience, a process seen as inevitable, even desirable. For such individuals the idea of the world from the beginning of history to the present day as having been predominantly subjected to the rule of satanic forces would have little appeal. And yet there are times when we all become aware of the intense suffering in the world and can feel the strong pull of what may best be described as negative forces. We may then well wonder how these originated and where in the world they are leading us. A former president of the United Nations General Assembly has given an answer in the clearest terms to the latter question when, speaking out of his experience in office, he tells us that few, if any, calamities have befallen the world without some advance notice and that "the end of man in our time may come as a rude shock, but it will no longer come as a complete surprise. The warnings given are there." Happily, an entirely different future for the world is being revealed, even though the time of confusion and suffering for mankind as a whole is not yet fully ended. We can, however, say that from now onwards those who listen to God and sincerely resolve to follow his directives are being assured by intimations coming to many sensitives all over the world that the time of their suffering is over and that they will share and participate in the glory of the New Age. It is in this sense that we may claim that the time of world restoration is at hand—a world physically restored and brought back into unity with God and alignment with the Cosmic Plan.

We may well ask, why only *now* is the physical restoration of the world to take place? What has been the cause of this long delay in the fulfilment of the Plan? It may sound almost too simple to state that the delay has been due to man's faithlessness and failure to recognize and respond to those messengers of God whose mission has been to urge upon man a reorientation of his will and to proclaim down the years the divine laws, through the observance of which alone he can live a life of happiness and peace in unity with all creation. Yet this is as close to the truth as any explanation capable of being given in another form or language.

It is also evident that with man's failure to control the destructive forces within himself, linked with the availability of nuclear energy, the restoration of the physical world must take place now if it is to take place at all. The essential counterpart of limitless power is the consciousness of limitless love and the good news of our day lies in the signs which are being given us, despite everything negative daily being brought to our attention. Messengers of God in many forms are amongst us at this time and his Love is being outpoured in abundance through them and also directly into the hearts and minds of men and women all over the world. Indeed, one of the most reassuring signs of our time is that God is no longer communicating exclusively through chosen mediators—though this is still a necessary and significant means by which he is reaching us—but his Love and his Will for individual and collective man are today being made manifest on an unprecedented scale through direct contact and in unmistakable ways to those who offer him their devoted hearts and minds.

Apart from the masters and spiritual teachers who move in our midst and whose task it is to awaken, inspire and prepare mankind for the dispensation of the Aquarian Age and for all the changes which are inevitably associated with the end of one cosmic epoch and the beginning of another, a significant approach is being made to our planet from beings of other realms and other planetary bodies. In previous chapters we have mentioned the widespread telepathic communications which speak of directives from the universal God to our cosmic brothers on other planets involving them in offers of assistance as we move rapidly towards a supreme planetary crisis. There is unquestionably an impingement from other realms upon our three dimensional, five-sense world which is exercising our scientists in a furious controversy. While some of them still prefer to ridicule and discount the widespread reports connected with sightings of Unidentified Flying Objects, other scientists of repute both in America and Russia are calling for global research into "the greatest scientific problem of our time." Appearing before a special committee of the House of Representatives in July, 1968, Dr. James E. McDonald of the University of Arizona's Institute of Atmospheric Physics said "the possibility that we are under surveillance is one I take very seriously." He added that it was in fact the possibility he believed to be most likely. "There is" (this scientist is reported as saying) "too much consistent evidence that we are dealing with machine-like devices." Referring to the great New York power failure which occurred on 9th November, 1965, Dr. McDonald stated that hundreds of reports of UFO sightings had been brought to the notice of the Federal Power Commission and that the source of the pulse which triggered the safety mechanism had not been identified.

Meanwhile telepathic messages, seemingly emanating from beings of other planets, show concern at what is seen to be a build-up towards a third World War and the way in which nuclear explosions in the northern hemisphere would inevitably upset the angle of inclination of the earth's axis through some melting of the icecap at the North Pole and the effect this would have on the amount of centrifugal force developed. There is also seen to be the possibility that our experiments with nuclear energy could affect other parts of the universe and it is these considerations which would seem to have a bearing on the theory supported by Dr. McDonald that our planetary activities are under observation by intelligences from outer space.

On the more positive side we are being assured in many of these telepathic messages that higher wisdom and spiritual and material aid are available and will be given in the hour of our greatest need. Mention has been made of the Ashtar Command as being the name given to the overall spiritual operation under the Cosmic Christ as its supreme head. It has been described as a hierarchical system consisting of beings from other dimensions who are wholly dedicated to the service of planets in our solar system, the focus at present being the planet Earth. These beings include those from highly evolved planets and those whom we would call ascended masters, and angels. The messages indicate that the planet Earth is being watched and guided as it undergoes its transition and moves into a new position in the universe in the course of its zodiacal progression, and that it is only as sufficient Light and Love are generated in the hearts and minds of mankind that this can be accomplished. The immediate work of the Ashtar Command lies in helping to prepare mankind to function in the new vibrational frequencies and to join the Galactic Federation.

As a result of the immense amount of spiritual and group work connected with the New Age which is now spreading all over the world, there is occasional evidence of misunderstanding on the part of groups in relation to the significance of the work being done by others, while some who prefer to keep free of group activity and work alone as individuals are unable to understand why so much weight is being attached to the need for an expansion of group work during this time of preparation for the changes—which to an extent at least are already upon us. In Chapter Seven we gave extracts from the Gildas teachings and the following message given by Gildas at a group meeting held in July, 1968, is particularly illuminating:

"We rejoice at the spreading of work in groups. Where two or three are gathered together much is created which we can use in the great struggle of the Light with the Darkness. Throughout the world power increases for both sides. Power increases for the Light, much is given, much received, much created, but this development is paralleled among those whose ways have led them to work in darkness. Light *will* triumph at last, of this there should be no doubt, but he who deceives himself that the struggle is already won, or that victory will be effortless, is either spiritually blind or a fool.

That which you struggle with in your own lives is but a reflection of what is being done for the world. What you gain for yourselves, you gain for humanity. Every step forward into harmony, peace and understanding in your lives carries forth reverberations and reflections into the growth of all that is for good and light in the cosmos. It is so easy to feel small and alone and as though what is being achieved with much effort for one little individual, in one small moment of space and time, is without value. None of these feelings is valid; that which you achieve is mirrored and magnified and forms part of the great throbbing force of light and positive life which shall be the saving of the world.

An individual working alone thus achieves much, but when the effort is made to work together in groups the mirroring effect is magnified many times, for each member mirrors the achievements not only of himself but of the others with whom he is linked."

A short while later, on 14th August, 1968, Gildas elaborated upon the same theme, saying:

"As people on earth are brought up in different cultures, different social settings, conditioned to different areas of belief, so there must be a need for different aspects of the teaching to be put through in different ways. All may not be to the taste of any one individual, yet all are necessary that the greatest possible number should feel their hearts and minds moved and attuned to the realms of the spirit.

Now at this time it is becoming increasingly necessary that each group with its own idiom should seek faithfully to understand the basic truths which are appearing to, and being given out by, other groups. It is essential that destructive criticism should end and that all should unite basically and realize that, though in different ways and along different paths, all are walking in sincerity to the same goal, and that when that goal is reached the one final truth shall be known and there will be a unity which comes without effort because of a new dimension in vision and understanding."

On 27th August, 1968, Gildas summarized his views on individual and group contributions as follows:

"There can be no blueprint for life as the world approaches the great and powerful entry into the New Age; but those who would wish to be most fully instrumental in the work would do well to endeavour to understand the many contributions which are needed in every aspect of life. Each individual, each group, must come along its own path and each one who opens himself to guidance shall be used to the fullest possible extent. When at last the fourth dimension is glimpsed, then shall each member of the corporate body see his contribution to the whole and know that without the part which he is playing there would be no whole, the pattern would be imperfect. None can be done without. Each contributes— once awakened to the need and open to guidance—to the full for the great cause. When the fourth dimensional state is reached, each individual and each group will realize not only the fullness of his own contribution but that of each other group and individual in the pattern and, instead of war and jealousy and strife, there will be a great peace where all will know the certainty and worth of the contribution which each is making to the one great work, the one great Light.

Before the fourth dimension can be reached, however, there is a great value to be gained from the linking of groups, the seeking to understand each other's purpose and contribution on the third dimensional level. This is difficult, but with tolerance and open hearts understanding will awaken and grow. Remember always that that which has been begun on the third dimension shall leap more readily into the fullness of blossoming on the fourth. Where preparation has taken place on one level, waves have gone out to other levels, establishing channels and beginnings which will thus be ready when the moment shall come and which will ease the difficulty of the moment of change.

Seek then from each other, to know and to understand and begin to build and form the links which shall in the fullness of time be seen to be vital to the perfection and establishment of the New Age."

Those who are acquainted with the subject of astrology will in no way be surprised at this emphasis on the significance of group activity as we enter the Aquarian Age. From now onwards it will be increasingly evident that association in groups and communities, large and small, governed by laws and values orientated to a spiritual pattern, will be one of the principal ways in which the dawning of the new dispensation will be made manifest. Indeed, it is impossible to over-estimate the importance of gaining a clear understanding about this trend towards group living and the reason for it, and we give below the text of a message through Elixir of the Findhorn Foundation, whose series of booklets "God Spoke to Me" will be known to many:

"As the darkness increases, so shall the light from all the Light Centres all over the world become stronger and shine forth in the darkness like beacons of light drawing My children of Light from all directions to the Centres of Light. You have a specific function to perform which can only be done as you draw apart from the chaos in the world. Let each Light Centre realize that it holds a great responsibility and follow out My directions to the letter.

Many Light Centres which have been lying dormant will waken up out of their slumbers and begin to function and many souls will be drawn to them. What you are doing here at this Centre of LIght many will be doing in the days to come. You are pioneering a way of life under My direct guidance and all is very well. Be not concerned as things grow worse in the world: they must grow worse before they can become better. Be still, be silent in your hearts, your very minds. Let the storm rage all around you but be not moved. I am with you always.

As I have tried to make clear to you, no longer can little groups and communities and individuals work on their own as they have done in the past, becoming more and more insular. There must now be a constant expansion, a linking together. It may appear like unity in diversity because you all have so many different and differing ideas but you will find, when they are all carefully linked together in My divine Love, that they will fit in perfectly.

Your work here is to do the linking together. You must never be dogmatic but absolutely open and free, willing to listen to all and glean the truth from each one. Remember there are many spokes which lead to the hub and every spoke is necessary to make that wheel strong and well-balanced, so never try to take one away. Simply accept that each is necessary and do not interfere with it but incorporate it into the whole, realizing that at the hub there will be no separation whatsoever. Keep your eye on the hub—unite in the things you can unite in—and ignore the things which cause division. Simply know that the time is near at hand when all those on their various spiritual paths will join together at the Source and find absolute peace, unity and harmony, for All are One in My sight. All are part of My Perfect Whole.

Each follow your individual path which you know is for you. Do what you know you have to do but never close your heart and mind to another who is on another path. Be very tolerant and do not reject something because you cannot understand it or accept it yourself. It takes all sorts to make a world. There are many facets to a diamond and every facet has its specific part to play. Lay all before Me and let Me throw the light of truth onto every aspect, then go ahead in absolute confidence linking all the different aspects together.

Let My peace and love infill and enfold each one of you. Let your lives be a song of praise, joy, glory and thanksgiving. Again let Me remind all Light bearers to unite and shine forth under My banner. United you stand, divided you fall. Victory is yours as you do My will and walk in My ways. Peace be unto you."

The foundation stone of Auroville (City of Dawn), a creation of the Mother of the Sri Aurobindo Ashram, Pondicherry, 2. India, was laid in February, 1968. Auroville has attracted wide attention throughout the world, envisaging as it does a "truly planetary university" and housing, education, work, food, leisure and a creative environment for 50,000 people from all walks of life and from all countries—"an experimental town, a laboratory of consciousness, a place in which to try out new ways for men to live together." Those concerned with this project are known as "Friends of Auroville."

It has been indicated throughout all our writings that the immensity of this vast cosmic operation which in one way or another involves every one of us requires many channels and instruments to bring it to completion. If we are truly on the threshold of events of universal magnitude, how in this context do we evaluate the invocatory plea, "May Christ return to Earth?" Does this merely, as some will maintain, portend the birth and growth of the Christ spirit within great numbers of individuals, leading to what Father Teilhard de Chardin would call the Christification of mankind—the ultimate divinisation of the world? The statement by Shri Krishna to be found in the Lord's Song, the Bhagavad Gita, is a reminder of the Christ's universality:

"Whenever there is a withering of the Law and an uprising of lawlessness on all sides, *then* I manifest myself. For the salvation of the righteous and the destruction of such as do evil, for the firm establishing of the Law, I come to birth in age after age."

Preparation for the ushering in of the Golden Age and for the events attendant upon its brith may require the physical presence at this time of many Great Ones, whose forms upon earth may be likened to the spokes of a great wheel whose hub lies in another dimension of time and space where all the "spokes" unite in the heart of the Cosmic Christ. Only with some such picture in mind—and no analogy is wholly satisfying—is it possible to obtain glimpses into the truth of the more mystical statements given in the Universal Link Revelation:

> "I am the Truth, the Light, the All throughout the Universe.

> Many will see aspects of Me in many forms, all of which are throughout the fullness of Me.

> My Whole Self is never divided.

> To effect My Materialization I require many instruments and this will create, to an extent, confusion..."

We must not therefore be surprised or unduly disturbed by the various Messianic claims being made in our day. This has been prophesied and in this connection we do not necessarily need to speak of anti-Christs. "By their fruits shall ye know them" and what matters is our own evolution in Christ consciousness and the recognition we find ourselves according to others who are claiming to do Christ's work. Peter's sudden outburst, "Thou art the Christ, the Son of the Living God!" is not without its deep significance. We may recall that Jesus turned to Peter and told him he was a fortunate man because it was not his own nature but the Father himself who had revealed this truth to him.

And so it is in our time that we need to pay particular attention to what is being revealed to us beyond the confines of our mortal minds. There is an Indian saying that "the mind is the slayer of the Real" and we repeatedly have confirmation of the way in which our critical and analytical minds limit and impede our growth in spiritual understanding.

While bearing in mind all we have said above, we think our readers would be particularly interested to know of some of the remarkable visions and revelations which sensitives are being given in connection with Sun Myung Moon who lives in Korea but who is reportedly appearing and teaching in spirit form in many different parts of the world. The circumstantial evidence of this from our own investigations is overwhelming and information about his role in the Cosmic Plan is being given independently to sensitives who have no direct connection with his physical form nor with his movement—the Holy Spirit Association for the Unification of World Christianity—which is spreading to many countries at this time. Earlier in this chapter we made reference to the Ashtar Command as being a hierarchical system under the Cosmic Christ, and we can only report that a number of sensitives have significantly linked the name of Sun Myung Moon with this system. While we were at Findhorn in the summer months of 1968, a visiting sensitive who had no previous knowledge of the mission of Sun Myung Moon was awakened early on 30th July, with words which puzzled her so much that it was only with reluctance that she was able to bring herself to share fully with us the clear message which had been given her. It was as follows:

> "Sun Myung Moon is direct link with Ashtar Command. Through him the forces are dispersed where necessary. These forces are not of one planet alone. They are gathered from many and are the chosen ones for this work for their knowledge and for their great love for the universal God."

Knud Weiking, the Danish sensitive associated with the work of the Universal Link at Borup in Denmark, has had it revealed to him that at a crucial moment in the changes coming to the earth—when the veil is rent with the realms of spirit—Sun Myung Moon will be used to unify the consciousness of the many whose minds will at this moment be opened to telepathic impulses.

From our own personal meetings with Sun Myung Moon, and from the inner understanding given us about his universal mission, our abiding impression is of one who acutely reflects the intensity of the burning flame of the Father's heart and wants all to share his mission—the mission of the Christ—for the redemption of the whole of mankind and the restoration of the physical world. We have spoken of the universality of the Christ in his appeal to all people at this moment of unprecedented challenge and opportunity and it is in his own conscious acceptance of this mission that Sun Myung Moon has meaning for the world. It is the need for urgent, immediate and sustained action in the service of the universal Christ which remains our predominant and enduring thought and inspiration as the result of our meetings in Korea with Sun Myung Moon.

We would like to conclude with the following extracts from a message given to Elixir on 26th August, 1968:

> "Where there has been complete darkness there will be great light. Where there has been hate, jealousy and resentment, tremendous love will flow. Where there has been dogged resistance to change you will see changes taking place overnight. Expect all this to come about; be ready for it and welcome it with open arms. Do not let there be any resistance found in you. Change your thinking and you will change your whole outlook. This can happen with your attitude towards a person or nation, the world. Open your hearts and let the love flow freely and watch all difficulties being overcome.
>
> Love is the greatest uniting factor in the universe. When you can approach every situation with love in your heart, all difficulties will be overcome in the end and all barriers pulled down. It may take time, but it will take place. So approach every situation

with purest love—My divine love. Always remember you are My hands and feet and I have to work in and through you My wonders to perform and simply know that with Me nothing is impossible. Radiate love to all your fellow men, see all as one great family, for all are one in My eyes. When I ask you to love all, I mean ALL. Therefore take all individuals, all nations, the whole world on your heart and love, love, love and see My Kingdom brought down here upon this earth."

Chapter Nine

Radioactive analysis of the substances brought back in the Apollo 11 space craft have established the age of the moon as being between 3,000 and 4,000 million years and the examination of these materials is making its contribution to the overall reappraisal of the origin and nature of the universe which is taking place in our time. Indeed, in many respects we find ourselves in the midst of something greater and infinitely more far reaching than the Copernican Revolution, when many long held and respected scientific theories were upset. We need to open our minds to all manner of new possibilities in regard to the universe and our position within it.

It is interesting to recall that when the genius behind the Apollo moon project, Dr. Werner von Braun, was asked how he evaluated the importance of putting a man on the moon, he answered: "I think it is equal in importance to that moment in evolution when aquatic life came crawling up on the land. It will cause a new element to sweep across the face of this good earth and to invade the thoughts of all men."

This remark reflects the kind of vision we all need to have in the times in which we live. We are on the threshold of a completely new evolutionary development—one could rightly term it a "leap" in evolution—which may indeed be compared with that epoch-making moment of the emergence of life from the oceans or with that equally historic moment when *homo sapiens* burst into existence as a new species. Our minds need to be capable of a similar "leap" if they are to measure up to the possibilities of contact with life in the universe in new and no double unexpected forms.

Indeed, our scientists are seriously envisaging the possibility of supra-civilizations existing in outer space, comprising entire solar systems, groups of stellar systems and whole constellations of stars. There is substantial evidence that from some of these systems in the depths of interstellar space we are receiving signals in the form of incredibly powerful artificial radio emissions. Let us consider for a moment the implications of the following observation which appeared in a leading article in the "New York Times" and which referred to quasi-stellar radio sources ("Quasars"), those titanic blazing objects which are defying all attempts to classify or explain them: "Has man finally made contact with the space communications network of the advanced galactic civilizations whose existence has long been suspected but never demonstrated?"

This question is much to the point and can no longer be ignored. In fact the well-known astronomer of Cambridge University, England, Professor Fred

Hoyle, does not attempt to ignore it. He tells us that we must be prepared to find in outer space creatures very much like ourselves, that for billions of years in the galaxy an interchange of communication has been going on, on a vast scale, and that we are as unaware of it as an uneducated native of the forests of Africa is unaware of radio messages. He envisages the time when we shall get ourselves linked up with this communications system. We shall then, as it were, have a "dialling system" to another planet and through a relay system be able to pass messages to the nearest star and beyond.

Now, if we ourselves can already hold a vision of this magnitude, is it not logical to suppose that more highly evolved intelligences in outer space may long have been transmitting messages capable of being received and interpreted by us once we have found the key?

It would seem that this conjecture is reflected in an international scientific project pioneered by Professor Rudolph Pěsěk of the Czechoslovakian Academy of Sciences. Professor Pěsěk in answer to specific questions expressed it as being his view that higher intelligence existed elsewhere in the universe and was conceivably seeking to communicate with us. The international symposium in question is called C.E.T.I. (Communication with Extra-terrestrial Intelligence) and involves scientists from America, Russia, Czechoslovakia, Scandinavia and other countries. It has the backing of the Soviet Academy of Sciences.

A book was recently published in America called "Cosmic Mysteries of the Universe" (Parker Publishing Company of West Nyack, New York). The author, Dr. Adrian Clark, is a respected authority in the field of space vehicles and rocket propulsion and was influential in developing the Vanguard satellite launching programme. He is closely linked with American space initiatives. In the introduction to his book Dr. Clark expresses the view that early man may have been under the instruction of extra-terrestrials of unsurpassed intelligence and he goes on to say: "If extra-terrestrial men were directing the early development of life on earth, it has special significance for this generation which is attempting to become interplanetary travellers." Dr. Clark adds: "The sightings of unusual flying objects today may be evidence of God's helpers who are watching, protecting, intervening as required to carry out God's Plan and hopefully preventing man from destroying himself and all other life on this planet."

In considering the question of Unidentified Flying Objects we have to appreciate the sharp division we find among scientists today in relation to the issue of extra-terrestrial intelligent life. It is a very different matter accepting the possibility of communicating with intelligences elsewhere in the universe by means of an advanced form of radio astronomy and acknowledging a link between objects seen in the sky and these intelligences. A number of scientists recognize the first without giving any kind of credence to the second and many scientists still dispute both. On the other hand, numbers of intelligent citizens throughout the world are pressing with increasing insistence for a satisfying explanation for many hitherto unexplained happenings taking place in the earth's atmosphere. It is no longer possible to suspect that college professors, medical men, clergymen, policemen, trained observers in weather, air and astronomy, commercial pilots, military groups, naval officers, lawyers, in addition to thousands of sound-minded, keen-eyed citizens, are all suffering from various degrees of hallucination. Russia's most learned planetary physicist, Professor I.S. Shklovsky, joint author of the scientific study "Intelligent Life in the Universe", in 1959 told the Soviet Academy of Sciences that one of the satellites of Mars, Phobos, was actually an artificial satellite, probably made of aluminium or magnesium. Before long space probes will prove or disprove the accuracy of this statement which is mentioned here on account of its interest and what it might imply. "We have to assume", said Dr Shklovsky, "that Phobos is hollow inside, something like a tin can from which the contents have been removed. It is an artificial satellite of Mars."

The two Martian satellites, Phobos and Deimos, were discovered by an American astronomer, Asaph Hall, in 1877. They behave in ways which are impossible according to known laws of astro-physics. Deimos orbits Mars in less than eight hours — in less than a third of the time it takes for Mars to rotate only once on its axis. Some of the finest scientific minds claim we can assume that intelligent beings on Mars must have constructed and placed these objects into orbit more than 2,700 years ago. An American astronomer, Dr.H.M. Stinton, of Yerkes Observatory, Wisconsin, recently told the American National Academy of Sciences : "Phobos may be a huge orbiting city filled with men, women and children. The other moon, Deimos, might be one too." And Dr. Fred S. Singer, one of the American Mars probe scientists of the National Aeronautics and Space Administration of the U.S.A. (NASA), agrees with this view and adds that the primary purpose of these artificial satellites would probably be to sweep up the radiation belts around Mars to enable Martians to operate in space without radiation hazards.

Since the earliest times, in both tribal and national histories and in the scriptures of the great religions, references are to be found to winged messengers, angelic beings, space chariots, discs of varied shapes and fiery wheels descending from the skies. But for long years man in his materialistic and limited thinking has tended to dismiss all these stories as myths and as not being worthy of credence. However, now that man is himself moving into space he may with advantage take a closer look at these stories. It is at least logical to assume that throughout our huge universe in which this planet is a tiny speck there are some more highly developed civilizations which have conducted broad explorations in space. A Russian scientist, Dr. E. Fyoderov, stating this conclusion in an article printed in Krasnaya Zvezda, the newspaper of the Soviet Ministry of Defence, criticizes those who scoff at suggestions that the earth may have been visited by inhabitants of other planets. He expresses the view that explorers were in the region of the earth long before life arose in the form that we know it.

It is relevant here to mention how the term "flying saucer" came to be used in modern times to describe these objects observed in the skies from time immemorial. In June, 1947 a private pilot, Kenneth Arnold, saw nine strange objects flying silently in formation past Mount Rainier in America. On landing he described what he had seen, saying that they looked to him like flying saucers. It was then that the modern wave of UFO sightings began and has continued to this day in the midst of growing controversy. These objects have been tracked on radar as travelling at the speed of 18,000 miles an hour and more, and there are thousands of witnesses in many countries who claim seeing these objects travelling at quite fantastic speeds and sometimes as disappearing in a flash as if moving into another dimension beyond the range of our vision. In recent years so much interest has been aroused by reports emanating from citizens all over the world and from all walks of life that Colorado University in the U.S.A. was officially commissioned to carry out a scientific investigation. The result was in many respects inconclusive and largely negative, but reports continue to flow in unabated and scientists both in America and Russia are pressing for global research into what many are coming to regard as the greatest scientific problem of our time.

It is often asked whether the astronauts have seen extra-terrestrial space craft and it is understandable although deplorable from the point of view of the ordinary citizen that much of the information which many feel should be made publicly available is regarded as being in a top secret category. There is, however, the report that astronaut James McDivitt, during his Gemini 4 space flight, took several photographs of a UFO about 20 miles away. He told the ground control station that it was "closing fast" and we then heard no more.

There is also, however, a most interesting and rather more detailed report by astronaut Gordon in the course of the flight of Gemini II, September 1966, and a coloured photograph taken by the astronaut appears on the cover of the American magazine Science and Mechanics for the month of June, 1969. His own remarks are quoted as follows:

"We were going south-east forward, heads forward in orbit. It came from our left and down below us. In other words it came into view from our left window, flew out in front of us. It looked just like space craft look when they're flying. We knew it was another space vehicle of some kind. But we had no idea of what kind, so we just grabbed the camera and snapped a couple of quick colour pictures of it. It was a sort of yellow orange. It looked just like the way the sun reflects from most metals up there. It had to be made of something like a metallic material to reflect light the way it was doing. There was nothing we could distinguish as having shape. It was about 50 miles away."

What evidence exists that space craft from outside our planet have actually landed upon the earth? In answer to this question it may fairly be said that an impressive amount of evidence has been reported in newspapers and journals in a number of countries during recent years. Not only have landings, apparently of extra-terrestrial space craft, been widely witnessed by reliable observers—of craft which are seen usually to "take off" and move quickly out of sight when humans approach them—but unusual markings are being discovered which could be related to such reported landings.

A case was reported from Villpula, about 200 miles north of Helsinki, Finland, in September, 1969. We were able to visit the scene within two weeks of the discovery of the markings by the owner of the property. The markings were precisely circular in appearance and consisted of a band, 40 centimetres wide, of apparently dead grass and vegetation, enclosing a circular piece of land 13 metres in diameter. This land was seldom visited and is approachable only through a wooded area along a narrow footpath. There appears to be no normal explanation for the condition of the vegetation and subsoil in the affected area, which have.been found responsive to a geiger test. A preliminary examination of the soil and vegetation strongly points to the affected area as having been subjected to some kind of radiation. This case is not dissimilar to other cases being reported in which the circumstantial evidence would seem to favour the hypothesis of contact with some kind of extra-terrestrial object.

The subject of extrasensory perception is one which is today being treated with increasing respect and was discussed in a scientific symposium held in 1969. Both American and Russian scientists envisage the possibility of perfecting telepathic techniques to the point where they can be used to keep contact with astronauts in the event of the electronic communications breaking down. Dr. I.M. Kogan of the Popov Institute of Studies in Radio-Electronics and Communications, Moscow, suggests that the human body generates between four and five times the amount of electricity needed for telepathy across long distances. He states that *in theory telepathy can occur over unlimited distances.*

Might not this promise of the scientists have a bearing upon the considerable number of reports already being received from different parts of the world that sensitive individuals are receiving messages allegedly originating from intelligences of other realms and other planets in the universe?

Chapter Ten

In the context of the theme of this book we may recall that down the ages man has tended always to look towards some moment, some period in future time, when individually and collectively he might enjoy the experience of that state of enhanced happiness and fulfilment which ever seems to elude him. There is that irrepressible, surging feeling within the breast of man that somehow, in some way or other, we should be able to witness the fulfilment of the age-old vision of peace and goodwill among men within our respective nations and throughout the world.

In some countries idealists—when those concerned have not been blatant seekers after power—have brought about revolution after revolution aimed at reforming or changing laws or systems of government with a view to obtaining greater happiness for a greater number of people, but the outcome has usually been yet another revolution when the inevitable imperfections of those involved in the outworking of the new arrangements become evident and sooner or later new pressures reach their breaking point. Other countries have what are called general elections, or presidential elections, but as soon as a new set of pledges has been given and the initial excitement has subsided, we tend to find the basic problems of our lives still very much in evidence. So we complain and protest in a variety of conventional and not so conventional ways and look hopefully to a future which never seems to materialize.

Many have come, somewhat fatalistically, to accept life on earth as a vale of tears and sorrow and look to the prospect of some "after life" condition for an amelioration of the situation or as a means of providing them with the kingdom of their heart's desire.

Truly, the misguided thinking and self activity of human beings has brought us to the very limit of time. Many of the things which were considered "good" for humans are turning out to be not so good after all—quite "evil" in many cases—and something seems to have gone very much awry with human judgment and wisdom. How otherwise is it conceivable that sober scientists should be warning us that the world really will come to an end in a few years' time unless something is done quickly and on a massive scale to halt and to reverse the fatal trends for which our thinking and activity are responsible. By the 1980s we may be forced to wear breathing helmets in many parts of the world; in 25 years around 80% of all the species of living animals will be extinct; and in the same period of time man will, according to conservative calculations, have reached a world population of around eight billion, a figure which many ecologists regard as the "crash" point beyond which the natural environment will not be able to sustain life.

Many young people are announcing that they do not intend to have children either now or a decade from now and that this is one of the ways in which they feel they can best serve the interests of humanity in its present predicament. In certain overcrowded areas of the world the time is coming when the nuclear bomb will be seen less as a threat than as a blessed release. Even today, with three quarters of the world going hungry to bed and a third dying of starvation, the ever present threat of widespread annihilation is not everywhere the main concern. Even so, nuclear scientists are protesting to their governments that the spread of atomic power plants, presumably designed to be of service to mankind, is unnecessary and that existing ones already pose a monumental threat to health. Pollution and the spread of radioactivity are together liable by 1980 to be responsible for making it impossible for women to bear children.

Altogether, the outlook for the human race is dismal indeed. Man seems to be moving to destroy the entire earth and every living creature upon it and it is useless to accuse people of being alarmists. Many people in all countries throughout the world are very much alarmed, and they have good reason to be. This is a fair statement about the kind of future man appears to have in store for himself and any thoughtful analysis of the human situation must lead to the same general conclusion.

At last the realization is beginning to dawn in man's consciousness that the world is in the shape it is because of the shape man is in by reason of his stubborn reluctance to relinquish what he has come to regard as his right to determine the course of his own life. He certainly does have that right and he seems to be making a pretty good job of determining it. Down the ages man has consistently tried to achieve the impossible in attempts to make his environment and the world into what he thinks it ought to be while, with rare exceptions in the lives of individuals, rejecting any suggestion that he should allow a radical change to take place in his entire overall mode of thought and expression. By reason of this stubborn and consistent opposition to the manifestation of the higher expression which has always been present and available within him we now see around us the formation of a gigantic world compost heap. Of course, there is nothing wrong about a compost heap. A process of disintegration and creation is taking place simultaneously within it, as indeed is very evident in the world today, and there is a cycle working under perfect law towards its completion.

The individual, however, is confronted with a choice. It is the same old choice, but he would need to be extremely blind and possibly somewhat deficient in a sense of smell to be unaware of the implications of making a wrong choice at this particular moment in the working out of the cycle—a choice which could prove, to put it mildly, extremely disagreeable for him. For the consequences are now more evident to him than possibly at any previous time in history. Either he elects to involve himself in the process of the new creation developing in the midst of the decaying compost or he elects to identify with the decaying process and suffer the consequences. Viewed superficially, it may seem heartless not to try to arrest the decaying process in the compost heap, but a flash of enlightenment will help him to realize that this is as futile a way of spending his energy as would be his attempt to put his hair in order first thing in the morning by combing and brushing the mirror in which he is looking at his own reflection

Some of you will recall the report appearing in St. Luke's Gospel (Ch 13) of a discussion with Jesus regarding those caught up in personal disasters, and whether such individuals could be held to be more "sinful" than their fellows. Jesus categorically replied to the effect that no such distinction could be made and that those, whoever they might be, who refused to undergo a radical change of heart and of their whole outlook on life would, as he put it, "all likewise perish." One might suppose that were he present third dimensionally in the flesh today he would be saying much the same thing to all of us as also no doubt—could his voice be heard amid the turbulence of the general election—to the leaders of all the political parties involved and to those about to cast their votes for another round of human government. All are basically in the same position so far as God is concerned. How absurd, how senseless has been this endeavour to keep in separate compartments, however much we may seek to deny it, our spiritual or religious expression and understanding and the so called practical politics which to an ever increasing extent demand our attention in the pattern of our daily living and relationships!

Once we accept the existence of God, a design and control throughout the universe and a divine plan for our world, does it not appear somewhat inconsistent to view the manifestly self active endeavours of our statesmen, our politicians and of ourselves, in this professedly Christian country, regulating and controlling our lives as if no divine pattern of control existed? For man to attempt to build a kingdom of his own in the midst of the Kingdom of God— deliberately to cut himself off from the Government of God—seems so ridiculous an undertaking and one so inevitably predestined to end in ultimate chaos and disaster that it is small wonder that we frequently find ourselves questioning our sanity and the sanity of our governments!

One thing must be clear. Our present overall crisis has not been brought about simply as a consequence of the passage of time through some long historical processes. It flows *directly* from what is known as the "fall" of man and it might therefore be helpful to give this a little consideration.

There is the most wonderful symbolism in the Biblical story concerning the Trees of Life and of the Knowledge of Good and Evil in the Garden of Eden. Perhaps only now are we beginning to see with crystal clarity the striking relevance of this allegory to the seemingly insoluble problems which confront mankind today. Clearly man's emphasis upon, and search after, knowledge has brought him to the threshold of dangerously explosive situations both in an actual and metaphorical sense. In some fields of knowledge, such as in that of atomic science, the stream of new information made available is doubled every three or four years. This means that text books are already obsolete by the time they can reach the hands of the student. With growing pressures upon them, is it really surprising that we see students in a state of revolt in many parts of the world for this and for many other reasons almost too numerous to mention?

We have already spoken of the inability of man in his human wisdom and reasoning to judge, in the long term, what course is "good" for mankind and what might be "evil." In our individual lives we have so often with due hindsight found that the events or circumstances we judged at the time to be "evil" were in fact true blessings in disguise. This fallen way of functioning is a moment to moment activity and we do not need, and never have needed, to maintain ourselves in it. We are to forsake that tree completely and in risen consciousness to return to the Tree of Life, symbolic of all that will fulfil our needs and provide the solution to our every problem. To express it another way, in our long history all the untold misery, all the suffering, all the tragedy and disease of every kind to which man has been heir has stemmed from his refusal to heed the injunction *to leave the Tree of the Knowledge of Good and Evil alone.*

Human beings simply cannot judge these things. There are great numbers of so called "good" people throughout the world who with the best intentions simply want to take the *good* fruit of the tree and leave the *evil* fruit alone. But it is all being taken from the same tree and the so called good people and the so called evil people suffer just the same, and the result of all this for mankind as a whole has been first a steady deterioration and now an accelerating landslide towards chaos, destruction and death. It is somewhat late in the day to recall that, according to the allegory, it was the devil (could that be man's self active mind?) who told Eve that to eat the fruit of the forbidden tree would *make her wise* and up until this time man has been acting upon the devil's own assurance that if he ate of the fruit of the tree he would *not surely die.* God said exactly the opposite. Who are we to believe was speaking the truth?

Our schizophrenic, cancerous and utterly distraught civilization is clearly reflecting its lost contact with the Tree of Life. One of the features of cancer is a lack of order and control as individual cells of the body proliferate and multiply without regard to the needs and interests of the body as a whole. The population explosion is an example at another level of just the same malfunction—a symptom of the larger cancer which unless arrested must inevitably destroy the whole body of mankind.

It is quite evident what we need to do. But we are already living on borrowed time and the time for talk as a substitute for right action is past.

Evidently we must initially treat this as a personal and individual problem and we are fortunate that there is in fact only one problem and, broadly speaking, one answer to it.

The question is this. Are we ready to let man's world go and accept instead, right now, the world and the Government of God as an absolutely practical proposition? This means letting God's Will be done in our thinking, in our living, in our speaking and in our acting.

Some of us are bound to think, and understandably, that there is nothing very new about this question. That is true enough. The expectation, however, is that in this day there will be something new about the *response.* Any imagined difficulty about giving a positive response is born of the mind, of man's self will, and that is the very devil, and the same old excuse by which mankind has effectively delayed the coming of the Kingdom on earth throughout all past history. It has provided a good smoke screen to enable man to continue functioning in his own ineffective, fallen, self-willed way, but where has that been getting him?

Besides, there seems to have been a strange impression among a great many good, sincere Christians which hasn't helped the situation. Many have thought that by repeating over and over again—and it must have been said billions and billions of times—the phrase: "Thy Kingdom come, They will be done on earth as it is in heaven"—God would *do* something or other to give effect to this prayer *without* our needing to be willing to *allow* his operation to take form through the yielded instrumentality of our own hearts, minds and bodies. All God has ever desired of us is our willingness to *allow the Kingdom to come.* For His part He has done everything that needs doing and if we are not *experiencing* the Kingdom which it has been His good pleasure to give us, but are in fact experiencing something rather different, than that is our own fault and there is really nothing more that God can do about it until we change our whole approach. We need to be *able* to receive what has already been given us—what is already present in our midst.

Man was created for the specific purpose of providing a means for God's action in the world, and when facilities created for one purpose are used for another we cannot complain when the instruments in question get out of order and become ineffective in the service of that other purpose. Old Testament history, except for isolated individual examples, is the record of man's collective failure to provide that needed means of God's expression upon the earth. The main culprit has been man's ego, his self active mind, the devil incarnate in every man who has to be overcome in the Christ power. The way has been shown us, but this does not absolve us from a personal responsibility to allow our Christ being to repeat the pattern in each individual case.

For Christians Jesus Christ has a unique and special place in history but let it be clear that Christians have no exclusive claim upon him. It is salutary also for us to remind ourselves from time to time of that remarkable and memorable passage in which St. Augustine, one of the earliest Fathers of the Christian Church, proclaimed: "This which we now call the christian religion existed among the ancients and *was* from the beginning of the human race until Christ Himself came in the flesh, from which time the already existing true religion began to be called Christianity." The universality of the life and mission of Jesus has been acknowledged by Mahatma Gandhi, that great non-Christian, in the following words:

> "Jesus belongs not solely to Christianity but to the entire world, to all races and people. I know many who have never heard the name of Jesus Christ or have even rejected the official interpretation of Christianity who would probably, if Jesus came in our midst today, be owned by him more than many of us.

It was because of man's historic failure through his fallen consciousness and self activity to accept his true mission and relationship to God that Jesus came to serve as a *substitute body* for the whole of mankind, becoming as he did a visible, living demonstration of the true pattern of living for the whole human race; showing man the need to accept his true identity as a god being, whose inner core was vibrationally one with God Himself and who, by deliberately identifying with, and allowing through his being the expression of, the nature and character of God, would become a conscious means for the flow of that nature and character into the environment of the world. Can anyone imagine anything more totally worth while and fulfilling than to give our life for this purpose? — Surely not a "sacrifice" unless, knowing the truth of the matter, one still imagines there is something more worth while to be done with it! What a glorious sense of exhilaration and freedom in the very thought of it!

Jesus through his own example showed that mankind itself is "the only begotten Son of God," that man is himself the bridge by which the life-stream of God and the things appertaining to heaven may cross over into the world. Indeed, man decides for himself whether his experience shall be heavenly or, here in the world, the experience of hell. God's Government is present—"the Kingdom of God is at hand"—whether man accepts it or not. The Government of God is not eliminated simply because of the rejection of it. Man symbolically with arms outstretched represents the cross by which everything God has to offer may pass through into the world of man or be nullified and distorted by man in the world. Rejection simply brings man into an experience of hell and, according to his degree and intensity of response to the Love, Truth and Life of God, ever present within his own being, it always remains open to man to determine at any moment *what* he will experience. All too often man is found responding to his environment, which especially in these days can be a somewhat depressing experience.

It is really a question of whether we are going to be attuned to bad news or good news. The choice is ours. It is rather like tuning in to a radio station—

in this case radio station G.O.D. There is a programme continually going on, but when the dial isn't on the station one is inclined to pick up a lot of static. The best and quickest way to get rid of the unwanted static is to get the dial back on to the station again, but mankind acts like someone who becomes so concerned with the static and his reaction to it, that he overlooks the simplest and easiest solution.

Station G.O.D. is, of course, once we come to accept its existence, the point of integration for each and every one of us, irrespective of our superficial differences or religious affiliations. There is still a great deal of prejudice in regard to the word "religion" and I personally find the following passage translated from the French and extracted from an article appearing in a little paper in Algeria extremely helpful:

"In its essential and eternal truth religion is that which binds all mankind one to the other and to the Creator. It is love and communion: it is also wisdom and truth. It is at once individual, inner and universal. It rests outside dogmatic and sectarian beliefs, outside limited and detailed creeds. Religion is not an authoritarian organization, exclusive source of the salvation of souls; it is for each of us an individual discovery of what we truly are, what God is and what are the true links between Him and His creatures. Religion is in every person and the inner Light which guides; it is also Life in so far as it is universal, the Divine Life which spreads like a generous, abundant, inexhaustible blood stream throughout all creation. In it theological arguments vanish. Labels that divide and fanatacisms more or less bloodthirsty all disappear. Unity is its unshakeable foundation, and this unity generates, sustains and renews the rich and prodigious diversity of manifest worlds."

For all of the foregoing considerations, seen in the light of what appears to be going on around us in the external world today, all the chaos, misery, suffering, devastation and conflict—even if there is no truth in the concept that God is "dead" there might be some agreement in the idea that He has, at least to a great extent, been missing in action. One gets the impression, which you may perhaps share, that something rather more might be expected of Christianity than is apparent upon the earth at this moment. We need perhaps to develop a clearer understanding of what it means to be a conscious, active participant in the process often spoken of as the building or the forming of the Body of God, the Body of Christ, upon the earth.

Let us consider this together, because whether we are aware of it or not this is precisely what we have been created to become the means of manifesting, of expressing—not only Christians but all people everywhere. But some of us need to establish more clearly, more perceptibility, a pattern of expression into which others throughout the world may be drawn as they find themselves quite naturally responding to the need of the time and also as realization dawns in their consciousness as to the true purpose of their lives. Individually of course we have the freedom to accept or reject this privilege, but who would want to reject it when we really understand what it implies?

The Christ is the *pure expression* of God, and Jesus has shown mankind that pure expression. Jesus has shown us so clearly that within each of us dwells the same Spirit—the ONE which in himself he spoke of as "He that speaketh and doeth the works." Jesus was not speaking or acting for himself at all.

According to Jesus we are all god beings, yet there is One God, One Family, One Christ, namely the Christ Expression and Radiance of all god beings. This is our true identity. If we ever thought we were anything other than this we have been acting in a counterfeit manner, in a sense of false identity. No wonder there has been so much confusion and wretchedness on earth.

Jesus came to restore in us the sense of our true relatedness to God and as we accept our true identity and allow through us out into the world the expression of the Christ nature and character, we become true cells of the Living God upon the earth. Is this not a beautiful thought that, irrespective of the reappearance of the Christ in any other form, we are *ourselves* to become the new-clear light of the new-clear age of Love and Truth and Abundant Life? What a meditation on the coming of the Kingdom, the Second Coming, the New Age!

From the time of Abram, there has from the divine standpoint always been the offer extended individually and collectively to man of a Great Promise. Because of the outworking of cyclic patterns, which we see exemplified in the rise and fall of empires and civilizations, this is a time of tremendous opportunity for the whole of mankind. For the individual the question is whether he is prepared to acknowledge and respond to the historic promise of a new and glorious age and to assume the personal responsibility implied in becoming an active agent in seeing this promise fulfilled. Let us not involve ourselves in a muddled interpretation of humility in relation to this mission which is truly our own destiny. What purpose will it serve, so far as we personally are concerned, if the New Age comes fully into manifestation and we are not a part of it? To be a part of it we need to be *in* it, and *functioning* in it, *now.* We do not need more "signs" and our physical age is quite irrelevant. Abram was ninety-nine years old when told by God that from his seed would come kings and nations. Although he laughed when he was told a son would be born to him, he nevertheless accepted the promise and began to work and live within the pattern of it. We may do this, too. Indeed, if suffering is to cease in the world; if man is to stop crucifying himself and carrying on in a way God never intended for him; if a new creation is to come with a minimum of further suffering and misery, surely we shall be eager, enthusiastic, to accept *in relation to ourselves* this tremendous opportunity of active personal involvement in the divine outworking which shall be for the glory of God and which will be a blessing to the children of men.

During Solomon's reign the vision of man's true mission on earth was lost and the particular cycle begun with Abram came to an end. From that time there needed to be a vibrational build-up towards another peak opportunity for man. Although the mission of Jesus Christ has produced unique and remarkable repercussions throughout the subsequent history of mankind up to the present day it is only now, at this time, that the vibrational build-up is once again of the character and intensity that provides the possibility for universal restoration. But the outcome is still dependent upon man's response. In the time of Jesus and immediately afterwards no broad foundation could be established for making the Government of God effective upon the earth. The basic divine pattern and the same essential purpose remain.

If we think the task before us to be merely a matter of experiencing what is known as "personal salvation," we are failing to catch the larger vision—the Body of God taking form on earth through our yielded minds and hearts and being given the means of action through our physical facilities. It is not a question of going somewhere or other after what we call "death." It is a matter of letting the Kingdom of God—the New Age—manifest, through us, here and now, upon the earth. And is not this what we all want to see take place?

Some may believe that the power and effectiveness of Christianity has been weakened by the appeal to identify rather more with the cross and suffering of Jesus Christ than with the inspiration of his life, his teaching, his resurrection and his ascension. We cannot here enter into discussion about these matters, though there is one truth of the highest importance being revealed in our day in the consciousnesses of individuals. This may disturb some and by reason of its remendously energizing implications set others on fire with a new sense of empowerment and a heightened resolve to respond with every fibre of their being in fulfilling their role in the divine plan.

Throughout the ages man has received communications and revelations from the invisible realms and they come to us in much the same form and manner in present times. These revelatory communications are now disclosing that Jesus in fact accomplished his resurrection without experiencing physical death—that he overcame death in very truth and that this is the true pattern for man now entering the New Age. Man indeed was not created for physical death, but for resurrection, ascension and to be the means for the activity of God throughout the universe. It is a lie that death is "natural": man can, if it is his will, be completely freed from this binding concept. We are told "the wages of sin is death," which is another way of saying that the whole concept which has become such a reality in man's experience is linked with his fallen consciousness and expression. In his risen consciousness is revealed the truth that Life and nothing but Life Abundant and Eternal is the reality.

Since some of you may be hearing about the resurrection of the physical body of Jesus for the first time, I would like to share with you the following passage from one of the communications relating to this theme; and I think it should be clear that what really matters so far as you are concerned is whether or not you feel able from the point of truth within you to give recognition and acknowledgement to the truth expressed. In a matter like this our minds are not likely to be very helpful. The name of the channel of expression in this instance and the names of those who are receiving confirmation by direct inner revelation are unimportant. You may of course rightly assume that if I did not myself give recognition to the truth of what is being here conveyed I would not be taking the responsibility of sharing it with you:

> "It has been said that it was the psychic body of Jesus which arose from the tomb and which was seen by the disciples and by the women, and by those sitting in the upper room; that only a psychic body could enter a room because matter cannot pass through matter. We would differ from this statement. The physical body of the Beloved Master, which was spiritualized, brought to life and action again by the Spirit of Christ, could not die, could not decay. The power of the Perfect Son of God manifesting through the physical body of Jesus during his earth life had so spiritualized the physical atoms that they were immuned from physical death, or from decay. The Spirit giveth life, and if it permeates a human body that body cannot die. This is the truth and the life, and the hidden story of the inner meaning of the Resurrection.
>
> The hope centred in the Resurrection is concerned not just with survival after death, but with life in relation to the living God."

I have heard people expressing indifference as to whether or not Jesus actually died in his physical body on the cross, but surely it is not a matter of indifference so far as we are concerned. This information, being widely communicated at this time, may cause a reaction of disturbance in some of us. It then becomes a question of whether or not we are willing to be disturbed in our beliefs. We may be very certain of one thing. Truth is no respecter of beliefs, opinions, views, dogma or convictions held by human beings. But Truth is very much concerned with the revealing of itself as this time and we may rest assured that nothing that is not of the Truth will stand.

Although we do not at this moment need to give detailed consideration to conflicting scientific hypotheses in this connection, it is a somewhat strange coincidence—if it is a coincidence—that a short while ago there appeared in the columns of the world's newspapers references to a crucial difference of interpretation in regard to the markings on the Holy Shroud of Turin. As many of you know, this shroud is regarded by those who accept its authenticity as by far the most important relic of the passion of Christ Jesus and as being the winding sheet placed around his body when it was removed from the cross and placed in the tomb. It bears the imprint of the front and back of a body marked with the wounds of flagellation (some 121 lashes according to one estimate) and crucifixion. The marks are said to have been left by the blood and sweat of Christ Jesus himself. When an amateur Italian photographer was allowed to photograph the shroud in 1898 the result became famous, because when he developed his film and looked at his own negative he saw, with great emotion so it is said, the genuine positive produced by two negatives and since that time there has been a great deal more rational, as opposed to purely devotional, interest in the Turin shroud. An international foundation with headquarters in Switzerland now claims that a study of the blood marks appearing on the shroud shows Jesus to have been alive when taken down from the Cross and his heart to have been beating in the tomb.

Perhaps the most significant thing, so far as we are concerned, about the insights and revealed truths flooding into the consciousnesses of increasing numbers of individuals in our day, is that a hard core of them reveals that the true destiny of man is to attain resurrection and ascension while still in the physical body and by so doing to overcome physical death. These communications are simultaneously coming to us with others which intimate that this is precisely what Jesus, who is widely regarded as Representative Man, himself achieved.

Now is the time when all false ideas about religion are to dissolve to let the unimpeded circulation of the Spirit fire the hearts and minds of responding mankind and free him for participation in the one great enterprise which can give meaning and purpose to his life. Human history to this time has been a story of lost opportunities. Christianity has meaning today to the degree that those who profess and call themselves Christians, together with non-Christians, allow in themselves a real understanding of the ancient Jewish vision of universal messianism and are willing to respond to that identical vision through a personal acceptance of the promise and mission of the ages. Christ, whatever else may here be signified, means the God-Man—the True Man—as contrasted with fallen humanity, the sub-human state of mankind. An anti-Christ is one who says: "No! Not *me!*" when presented with the opportunity of becoming Christed—of becoming a true human being. This opportunity is open to all who are willing to give up their little lives and their petty preoccupations. Then: "Behold! I make all things new!" It is not a question of earning or deserving, of pride or humility, all of which appertain to man's self concern. It means an absolute yielding in utter selflessness of our entire being to allow God to enter in, to accomplish His work in and through the individual and out into the world.

How wonderful it is to know that the Kingdom of God, the Government of God, the Body of Christ, the One True and Universal Civilization of Man on earth, is taking form in us at this very moment, as we let the old order pass away!

UFOs and the Awakening of Mankind

The worldwide UFO phenomenon represents a challenge to man's understanding that it is neither reasonable nor wise any longer to ignore.

I would invite attention to "The UFO Experience—A Scientific Enquiry," by Professor J. Allen Hynek, the noted astronomer of Northwestern University, U.S.A., and former official adviser on UFOs to the U.S. Air Force. I regard this treatise as being essential reading material for those seeking the most authentic up-to-date scientific information on this subject.

In the concluding pages of his book, Professor Hynek observes that we may well be faced with what he calls "a new fact" about the universe, involving a scientific breakthrough of major magnitude calling for a reassignment and rearrangement of many of our established concepts of the physical world. In that event we would be confronted not simply with "a small step in the march of science, but a mighty and totally unexpected quantum jump."

I would like to make it perfectly clear that the "quantum jump" which I myself will be regarded as having taken, even perhaps exceeded, may appear as totally unjustified in the present thinking of Professor Hynek and his scientifically minded colleagues. But I unreservedly maintain that, in its approaches to the subject of extra-sensory perception, science is already making progress towards giving recognition to the validity of the means whereby the greater part of the information given in this chapter was received.

It is evident for all who are not entirely blind to the signs of the times that our planet is today undergoing an acute evolutionary crisis. We might equally call it a spiritual crisis. To the peoples of our divided world the choice would seem to be clear—to change our ways and unite, or to perish like the civilizations of the past.

Actually, it is not quite like that, because while the old and outworn civilization is doomed and dying there is already evidence of something new and glorious—a new man, a new creation—coming to birth. We are to experience this as a total healing—the welding into oneness—of our divided and tortured body of humanity.

There is, however, a need first to view our condition in its cosmic context, because we have entered into what may come to be known as the Cosmic Age, the Space Age, and I would like to offer you my understanding of what this means.

My understanding is that we each form part of a universe of living energy—an immense, unified field of living, pulsating energy; and if we are to speak of God, then God must comprise the totality of this universal life energy and must Itself be each and all of the manifestations within the universe in their countless forms, visible and invisible, and infinitely more besides, which the human mind cannot possibly comprehend. This Living Wholeness of Being is infused in its every part with a loving and purposeful Intelligence and moves consistently towards maintaining itself in order, harmony and balance, to maintaining its oneness and perfection.

It follows that man's mind is designed to be attuned to, and to keep attuned to this consciousness of oneness, of wholeness, of perfect being, and to experience this in conditions reflected in the environment, which would thus become, in metaphorical language, heaven upon earth. Yet we know that throughout recorded history the very opposite has been the condition most generally experienced on earth. In the place of wholeness, perfection, order and harmony, we have tended in ourselves and in our world to experience conditions of division, imperfection, confusion and conflict, which our newspapers, televisions and radios daily bring to our attention.

In the urgency of the present moment no good purpose is served by debating the reasons, associated with man's inbuilt power of free will, why humanity throughout history has clung to an apparently self-imposed course of suffering, conflict and destruction. The important thing now for us to realize and to accept is that energies are at hand, as indeed they have always been at hand, to help us to move out of this condition and we cannot afford any longer to ignore them.

The barriers in man's mind are in fact today giving way to powerfully creative and uplifting energies which are flooding into his consciousness to provide him, individually and collectively, with an unparalleled opportunity to be instrumental in bringing new life to the planet, a new civilization to birth upon the earth, a civilization based upon enduring values, qualitative values of love, truth, joy, peace and the ideal of service to his fellow human beings and also not least to the other life-streams which contribute to and support the life of our planet. These values have been proclaimed to man by wise ones down the ages, and now man is required to incarnate and express them ever more consistently in his daily living if he is to enjoy any future existence upon the earth. Many are the ways that are open to man to play his part in the creative process, and these energies themselves, provided he opens himself to them, are the enabling source to provide him with the strength to be increasingly effective to this end.

A new inward enlightenment, a resurrection, a breakthrough in the orientation of man's thinking, is coming about through a willing yielding on the part of man to the pressure of these creative and constructive energies which only appear destructive for those who seek to resist or ignore them, but are creative for all who are willing to give recognition to, and to serve, the overall and universal purpose. They give no support to old thought patterns based upon hatred, greed or self-seeking of any kind.

This orientation of outlook, which is beginning to be shared by increasing numbers of people, will have its counterpart in a great technological breakthrough, designed to move man beyond the tribulations and dangers of the nuclear age and to give him new understanding in the use of electrical energies capable of quickly cleansing the earth of problems relating to pollution, population and disease of every kind. These energies will totally revolutionize all forms of transport upon the earth and, indeed, affect the entire material and spiritual life of man.

You may well ask, on what authority can such a statement be given? It may be said in reply that this, broadly, is the core of the information stemming from higher levels of awareness now being imparted to the consciousness of man in different parts of the world—information which I have reason personally to accept intuitively as valid and I share it with you on this understanding.

These energies are a manifestation of the energies of transformation which are moving in our midst at this very moment.

There is one further piece of information I want to share with you and this relates to an operation within the spiritual order of the universe known as the Ashtar Command. Now the Ashtar Command is defined as being an hierarchical system under the Supreme Intelligence of the universe. It consists of highly evolved beings from the spiritual realms and beings from planets in our galaxy and other galaxies who have taken a commitment to make contact with as many minds of earth people as possible at this time through many different methods of approach to, and communication with, earth beings, including telepathy and various forms of ESP contact; also, on occasions, manifestations in the third dimension, that is to say, through physical contact A great proportion of the so-called UFO activity represents the operation of the Ashtar Command, whose work is to help in raising the consciousness of all forms of life upon earth as our planet, as a part of the solar system to which it belongs, moves in the course of its progression through the universe into a new position and comes under the impact of new cosmic energies.

In telepathic communications coming to the consciousness of many individuals at this time, the Ashtar Command is specifically inviting recognition both of its reality and of the high purpose of its mission, which is seen ultimately as the establishing of a universal brotherhood of life, dwelling throughout the universe in peace and the spirit of mutual service and co-operation under the One Supreme Universal Power.

I think we can all realize how inevitably this overall Plan embraces, even if it transcends, man's age-long dream of peace on earth and the brotherhood of man, and how each of us is being urgently invited to play our part in bringing this about, by allowing ourselves to be raised to a higher state of consciousness and being, so that we may daily more effectively live a true and authentic life. Only in this way shall we be enabled to participate in the over-all task of building one united civilization of man, in which man will find his true purpose of joyous, creative cooperative living in brotherhood and peace-ful communion not only with the other life-streams upon the earth but also with the created life forms of other worlds with which, as we move ever deeper into the Space Age, we are now to be joined.

In conclusion:

1.   We are being invited to accept what for many of us is a new fact, a new truth: that there are superior forms of intelligent life in the universe which are making contact with us by various means and in various ways.
2.   This intelligent life operating according to universal law and in the ser-vice of One Supreme Universal Power is working to implement a plan for peace and brotherhood throughout the universe, which of course includes our planet.
3.   The peoples and governments of the world can choose, individually and collectively, either to continue to strive towards a solution of the problems of the world as if our planet were an isolated unit, or we may enlarge our capacity to solve all our problems by giving recognition to and by cooperating with this higher wisdom and intelligence which is being made available to us.
4.   We have this free choice, but higher intelligence is informing us in tele-pathic communications that we shall not in fact be able to solve the many difficulties we are continuing to create for ourselves without our coming to think and live in a completely new way and without establishing an effective link, directly or indirectly, with the Higher Intelligence which governs the entire universe. We will then be given every assistance to solve all our prob-lems and to live a fully creative life in peace and brotherhood on earth and in harmony also with life throughout the universe.
5.   In cooperation with their governments, the peoples of the world have a vital role to play in bringing about a universal civilization, a true brotherhood of man, upon earth.

Appendix 1

Science and Absolute Values

The Third International Conference of the Unity of the Sciences

Founder's Address
Sun Myung Moon

November 21-24 1974
London, England

Honorable Chairman, distinguished scientists, eminent professors and scholars, I deeply welcome all of you who are attending the third International Conference on the Unity of the Sciences sponsored by the International Cultural Foundation. As I am sure you are aware, two previous conferences have been held: the first in New York in November 1972, and the second in Tokyo in November 1973. As the founder of the International Cultural Foundation, I have desired and done my best to create and maintain, throughout these conferences, an atmosphere in which an open and unreserved exchange of opinions could take place. And I have been greatly pleased with the fruitful results of these conferences and the participants who have contributed so much to them.

At the present time, more and more serious problems continue to develop and confront mankind. The solutions to these challenging problems call for and indeed require not partial and local approaches and ideals, but rather a global approach and the wisdom and knowledge of the many distinguished scholars gathered here at this conference.

As a scientist myself, I have been observing with keen interest the development of science and technology. I know that science and technology and what we call the "scientific method," have had a far reaching impact on human life.

Through observation and study of the world of reality, science has extended and expanded this reality beyond what can be perceived by our physical senses. We are cognizant of bacteria which we can detect only through a microscope. Some of us journey to the moon, directed by computers whose astronomical speed of calculation baffles the human mind, while others talk about making it an everyday possibility. To our naked eyes, the earth still appears flat, but science has compelled us to admit that it is round. A diamond appears to be solid but we were once amazed to know that in fact, it is a scattering of atoms whirling around in quite an empty space. On a more abstract level, the transition from reality to extended reality is described by the transition from classical to quantum mechanics and from the deterministic model to the probabilistic model, both of which are equally or more confusing to common minds.

Although the progress in science has provided us with a tremendous amount of information, we still suffer from our inability to internalize this information and our inability to fully comprehend its deeper implications. This inability has led to much anxiety, confusion and uncertainty, which results from a loss of a firm basis and standard of reflection. As a result, we feel that we are in a state of imbalance between ourselves and the suddenly expanded reality caused by scientific progress. Meanwhile, when we think of the strong probability of our finding in the spiritual world the answers to the disharmony and imbalance of the limited human function of thinking, it does not seem accidental that recently Zen and meditation and their practices have become controversial objects of scientific research in the West, as well as in the East where they have so long been practiced and valued. The study of extra sensory perception has drawn the attention of quite a number of scholars in the academic community. In particular, the discovery that a dolphin can communicate with human beings intelligently deserves notice. Along the same lines, it has been observed that plants respond to the love and other emotional states of human beings. These discoveries suggest that our present view that the animal and plant worlds are lacking in consciousness and reason may be limited. We may now as well envision a universe in which a harmonious co-existence may be brought about between human beings and other creatures, where man, being the center of all things, may serve as the spokes of the wheel turning the whole universe in ultimate harmony and oneness.

Other items worthy of notice are the roles of the educator and the medical doctor which may be drastically affected by the ability of the computer to treat enormous amounts of information accurately and promptly, Some scientists have hinted that the future study of elementary particles and cosmology may alter our concepts of space and time.

A study conducted by the Club of Rome informs us of the potentially disastrous events in the near future due to pollution, population growth, scarcity of natural resources and rapid industrialization. Recently it has been found that ozone is on the decrease, caused by repeated nuclear testing. As you all know, the presence of ozone in the atmosphere is indispensably vital to the survival of life on the earth, since destruction of protein molecules does occur in the absence of the ozone layer.

Solutions to these problems cannot be arrived at through the efforts of scientists alone, nor by the efforts of any particular individual, group or country. The study of the Club of Rome, previously mentioned, clearly indicates the finiteness of the world's resources and environs, and also makes clear the absolute necessity of a global approach and cooperative effort for proper and complete solutions to the world's problems. These problems call for a world view, accompanied by an attitude of sacrifice and cooperation among all peoples of the world, transcending the interest of any one community or nation. Such a spirit of cooperation will be attained only when all mankind view themselves as members of the same human family. This revolutionary change in human consciousness to such an idealogy has long been needed and is vital to man's survival today.

In most educational systems in every nation of the world, the merit of competition and the survival of the fittest, achieved only by the winners in the competition, has been overly stressed. This has long been the plague undermining the healthy human endeavour to lead mankind into the world of peaceful co-existence by bringing them to be members of one human family. Now mankind somehow has begun to feel that in educating people the emphasis should be shifted and cooperation be made vital for survival. In light of this viewpoint, the goals and philosophies of education will have to undergo a profound transformation.

In the past, we have recognized the contribution of science and technology to the enrichment of human life without deep reflection. Now we begin to wonder. Some disquieting questions come to mind. Are we happier? Are we ethically more sound? Are we becoming more humane with love and concern for one another? Answers to these questions are not found simply by analyzing statistical results because the human being has many aspects which are not discretely quantifiable. In any discussion of the quality of life, these nonquantifiable factors play a major role. As illustrations, let me cite love, the ideal, the joy of creating, belief in God, and numerous other value systems. The question of the preservation and development of these humane aspects of life remains the greatest theme of our research. In light of this theme the question of interpretation and proper use of the vast amount of information created through scientific research and discovery becomes a profound and serious one.

Our attitude which tends to overemphasize the value of science may need re-examination. A scientific truth is tentative—the truth in one generation being possibly denied in the next. Consistent results, derived from a model built on the basis of a limited phenomenon, constitute scientific truth. However, in the course of building a model we go through the processes of idealization, simplification and approximation. As a consequence, we may have an approximated truth, and not the absolute truth. Science has grown so big that it sometimes seems beyond the realm of human beings.

Science should be gravely thorough and rigorous in determining facts, but in the process of utilizing the information and achievements, science should retain its position as one of the areas of human creativity. It should stay within the human realm so that it may be used and controlled and appreciated like the works of art and music.

When we reflect on the history of the human race, we see that there have been new frontiers in every era, some culminating in the development of literature, and others in the blossoming of medicine or the other sciences. Yet in the past, development of science and technology has been aimed mainly at the conquest and exploitation of nature.

Today this very science compels us to set up a new ethical standard. The new ethic should concern itself with the problems of love for nature and a re-examination of human values and the need for cooperation among human beings. It should attempt to set a new view of value and a new ethical norm which can bring about an ideal world of harmonious co-existence among all creatures on the earth.

The development of science and technology has certainly raised issues that invite us to seriously reflect on what is essential for us to remain human and to preserve humanity in our lives. I strongly believe that all this can be made possible only when every field of scientific technology is mobilized for the benefit of mankind and when a cooperative spirit of human activity is available on the part of the men who handle the scientific technology.

I ardently desire and expect the answers to come from you. This will surely be realized by assembling the results of your respective researches with your opinion and wisdom. From the very bottom of my heart I beg you to play the role of the bridge that will connect and lead the present world to the world of higher dimension and absolute value.

Thank you for your attentive listening!

Appendix 2

New Renascence Charter*

We proclaim a new Charter of Life, a new inspiration to live, not in terms of outworn dogmas, but in the new truths that Life is revealing.

This Charter is for those who need to find a new means of re-union with Life: the Life that gave birth to creation, the dynamic Order that made and maintains the Universe. We believe that same Life is the birthright of man.

We do not obtrude a formal creed, but affirm the Life of a Living God, waiting for man's response; not a God afar off in a distant heaven, but Good that is ever at hand.

This is a gospel for men; no longer helpless dependants on an unknown Deity, but fellow-workers with the Powers that Be; not suppliants prone before a despotic God, but crusaders, erect and alert to co-operate with Life's Power.

We believe that Life is unending adventure: that God is the Good man needs; not the potentate of Paradise, but the Power of immanent Life; the Power that can be realised by any who have the courage to welcome each crisis as a challenge, an invitation to new adventure. Rather than contemplating failure we focus for success.

We believe in the evolution of a higher type of man; sane in the science of a Life-engineer who constructs with intelligence, yet human in sympathy earned through daring to take the unknown way. A man in all points tempted, yet not 'missing the mark'; who has plumbed depth and darkness, alone, in the strength of the Light of Life.

We believe that a *new renascence* is possible for man; a re-birth to a new dimension of Living—conscious and creative.

This we affirm is the Gospel of Christ, the Gospel of Man triumphant, who faced the challenge of the cross, and brought Life and Immortaility to light. For He was the pioneer of nature redeemed.

His character is the Living Creed which must now come true in the character of man.

He *proved* that God incarnate is Life's new testament for the world.

Ian Fearn

* By kind permission and courtesy of The New Renascence Fellowship.

The following addresses refer either to names mentioned within the body of the book or are among those with whom the writer has had personal contact and finds especially informative and/or challenging with regard to the need for new thinking and a change of consciousness:

Avalon Group
Castle House, Keinton Mandeville, Somerton TA11 6DX, Somerset, U.K.

Axminster Light Centre
Clinton House, Castle Hill, Axminster, Devon EX13 5RL, U.K.

Center for UFO Studies
Established to pursue a vigorous scientific study and to end a quarter century of misrepresentation and misunderstanding of the UFO phenomenon
2623 Ridge Avenue, Evanston, Illinois 60201, U.S.A.

Centro Studi Fratellanza Cosmica
Via Campiglio 3, Milan, Italy

Dena Foundation
4117 NW Willow Drive, Kansas City, Missouri 64116, U.S.A.

Emissaries of Divine Light
Sunrise Ranch, Loveland, Colorado 80537, U.S.A.

Essential Science
6508, E. Cactus Road, Scottsdale, Arizona 85254, U.S.A.

Fellowship of the Crown
P.O. Box 3743, Carmel, California 93921, U.S.A.

Findhorn University of Light,
Forres, Moray, Scotland, U.K.

Heralds of the New Age
Apt 7, 119 St Stephens Avenue, Parnell, Auckland 1., New Zealand

Holy Spirit Association for the Unification of World Christianity (HSA-UWC)
International HQ Belvedere, 7235 Broadway, Tarrytown, New York 10591, U.S.A.
44, Lancaster Gate, London W.2., U.K.

International Cooperation Council
17819, Roscoe Boulevard, Northridge, California 93921, U.S.A.

Institute of Crystal Truths (Munedowk Foundation)
Box 268, Route 1, Kiel Wisconsin 53042, U.S.A.

Lorian Association
A cooperative association of such individuals and groups who have as their
direction the demonstration of new vision and of the higher potentials of
humanity
P.O. Box 941, Belmont, California 94002, U.S.A.

Mark Age Publications
327 N.E. 20th Terrace, Miami, Florida 33137, U.S.A.

Mondcivitan Republic Servant-Nation,
27 Delancey Street, London NW1 7RX, U.K.

New Age Teachings
37, Maple Street, Brookfield, Mass. 01506, U.S.A.

New Renascence
Weald, Laughton, Lewes, Sussex BN8 6AH, U.K.

Open Mind Publications — Group New Age
c/o P.O. Phillips Road, Mahogany Creek, 6072, Western Australia

Planetary Citizens
777, United Nations Plaza, New York, N.Y. 10017, U.S.A.

Phoenix Institute
2404, Broadway, San Diego, California 92102, U.S.A.

Ramala Society
Chalice Hill House, Dod Lane, Glastonbury, Somerset BA6 8BZ, U.K.

Re-Education Association
2065 Sacramento Street, San Francisco, California 94109, U.S.A.

Spiritual Research Society (publishers of *Exploring the Mysteries of Life*)
740 Hubbard St, N.E., Grand Rapids, Michagan 49505, U.S.A.

United Kingdom Advisory Council for Human Development
Coordinates certain groups, associations and institutions concerned with
expansion of consciousness and general growth, maturity and development of human beings and relationship
16, Great Ormond Street, London WC1N 3RB, U.K.

Understanding Inc.
P.O. Box 494, Merlin, Oregon 97532, U.S.A.

Unité Universelle,
22, Rue De Douai, Paris 1X, France

Universal World Harmony
1, St George's Square, St Annes-on-Sea, Lancs. FY8 2NY, U.K.

World Goodwill
866 United Nations Plaza, Suite 566-7, New York, N.Y. 10017, U.S.A.

World Union
Sri Aurobindo Ashram, Pondicherry 2, India

Appendix 4

The Foundation for Peace through Unity

What It Is

A universal fellowship for promoting mutual understanding, transformation of the self and development of wholeness of being—with the aim of achieving a continuously higher quality of life to be given expression in practical, cooperative ways which lead to ever more intensive individual, group and community involvement in such unifying thoughts, feelings and activities as provide an indispensable foundation for enduring harmony and peace within, on which a state of dynamic, creative peace in the outer world must essentially be founded.

How It Functions

(1)   Through cooperation and linking with individuals, groups and organizations throughout the world having similar aims or aims consistent with the purposes of the foundation;

(2)   Through availing itself of facilities where individuals sympathetic to the aims of the foundation may participate in the necessary inner and outer work designed to increase their capacity as world servers and true emissaries of peace: these facilities at present consist of the beautiful eight acre estate of Gövik, near Gothenburg, Sweden and the five hundred acre estate of farmland, woodland and lake of Ramsjöhall, close by;

(3)   Through providing an environment ideal for developing an "inner listening" attitude to Life, together with opportunities for creative physical work, for mutual education and for participation in lectures, seminars and discussions;

(4)   By the printing and publishing of books, pamphlets and other material and by undertaking such travelling as may be thought necessary to further the aims of the foundation.

A basic book of the foundation, *Let Life Live,* translated from the Swedish by the author, Gita Keiller, in collaboration with Anthony Brooke, may be obtained at the cost of £1.20 ($3. U.S.A.), including postage, direct from the Mitre Press, 52, Lincolns Inn Fields, London WC2A 3NW.

Let Life Live contains insights on basic questions of universal concern, revealed to the author in deep meditation. Examples:

On equality

You are all equal in the right to be uniquely different expressions of Eternal Life.

Revolution

True revolution comes when one makes one's life an example to follow.

Freedom

Freedom, in the true meaning of the word, is to seek the laws behind all life, to find them, to obey them and in this way continually to enrich one's consciousness and one's universe.

Universal compassion

When you really feel "we", your true compassion will go out both to those who suffer and those who cause suffering. Your love will include the whole picture of suffering because, as you know in your heart, both parties suffer. . .

Discipline

Discipline is to listen . . . thankfully and joyfully to listen to the lessons which nature has to teach. It demands a discipline—a one-pointed attention—to learn to live life wholly and fully. It is for this reason one listens to, and learns from, the laws behind all life . . . which always lead to a continually greater degree of freedom.

Let Life Live contains much of vital interest to all who are concerned with true living, with the changing times and with the New Age.

For further information about the activities of the foundation, please write:

Foundation for Peace through Unity,
Gövik, 430 40 Särö, Sweden.

Peace Through Unity is a non-profit making foundation and is gratefully open to receive donations.